D1187367

HOLLY, YEW & BOX

HOLLY
YEW & BOX

WITH NOTES ON OTHER EVERGREENS

BY

WILLIAM DALLIMORE

[1908]

THEOPHRASTUS

SAKONNET

1977

First Edition 1908

(*London*: John Lane The Bodley Head, 1908)

First Reprint by Theophrastus Publishers 1977

(*Sakonnet*: Theophrastus Publishers, *P. O. Box 458,*
Little Compton, Rhode Island, 02837)

Library of Congress Cataloguing in Publication Data

Dallimore, William.

   Holly, Yew & Box.

   Reprint of the 1908 edition published by John Lane,
London, *New York.*

   Includes index.

   1. Holly.   2. Yew.   3. Box.   4. Ornamental evergreens.   I.   Title.

SB428.D34   1976   635.9'773'271   76-10174
ISBN 0 913728 12 8

PRINTED IN THE UNITED STATES OF AMERICA

ILEX ALTACLARENSIS.   IN THE ROYAL GARDENS, KEW

HOLLY, YEW & BOX

WITH NOTES ON OTHER EVERGREENS
BY W. DALLIMORE
AND 175 ILLUSTRATIONS
THE DESCRIPTIONS OF THE VARIETIES
OF THE COMMON HOLLY ARE BASED ON
THE MONOGRAPH BY THOMAS MOORE

LONDON: JOHN LANE, THE BODLEY HEAD
NEW YORK: JOHN LANE COMPANY. MCMVIII

Turnbull & Spears, Printers, Edinburgh

INTRODUCTION

THE usefulness of the various Hollies, Yews and Boxes for garden decoration, coupled with the fact that many of the best sorts are but little known, furnished the inducement for the preparation of the present work. At the same time it was considered advisable to append a descriptive list of other useful evergreens. With the exception of the Yews, Conifers have not been dealt with through lack of space.

The Hollies, Yews and Boxes, on account of their general usefulness, are dealt with more fully than other subjects, and in addition to descriptions of most of the best sorts being given, notes on cultivation and uses are introduced, with a selection of extracts from various works on the superstitious legends, poetry, etc., attached to each group.

As the most important group, the Hollies occupy the premier position. The "Common Holly" and its numerous varieties form a very extensive and varied group, which is treated as

Introduction

fully as possible, whilst attention is directed to other species, many of which are but little known. The descriptions of the varieties of Ilex Aquifolium, as far as possible, are those of the late Mr Thomas Moore, which appeared at irregular intervals in the *Gardener's Chronicle* during the years 1874, '75 and '76, the editor of that journal kindly allowing use to be made both of the descriptions and accompanying illustrations. A departure has been made from the usually accepted statement that "all the garden Hollies are forms of I. Aquifolium," and for various reasons it has been thought desirable to place some of the varieties under the Canary Island species I. platyphylla, whilst others are referred to as hybrids. Many of the leaf illustrations will be recognised by all who know *Moore's Monograph*; there are, however, numerous new ones, together with a selection of photographs of isolated plants and groups, all of which are the work of Mr E. J. Wallis.

In addition to the *Gardener's Chronicle* I am indebted to the following works, among others, for information and extracts :—Johnston's Botany of the Eastern Borders; Selby's British Forest Trees; Browne's Sylva of N. America; Evelyn's Sylva; Miller's Dictionary of Plants; Sargent's Forest Flora of Japan; Garden and Forest;

Introduction

Loudon's Trees and Shrubs; Floricultural
Cabinet; Parkinson's Theatrum Botanicum;
Holland's Translation of Pliny's History of the
World; Sargent's Trees of N. America;
Hanbury's Complete Book of Gardening;
Johnson's and other Herbals; Plant Lore,
Legends and Lyrics, by Richard Folkard, Jun.;
Cole's History of Plants; Strutt's Sylva Brit-
annicum; Allibone's Quotations, etc. Thanks are
also due to various nurserymen and others for
specimens and information received.

W. DALLIMORE.

ARBORETUM,
ROYAL GARDENS, KEW.

CONTENTS

THE HOLLY

THE YEW

ix

Holly, Yew, and Box

LIST OF ILLUSTRATIONS

xi

Holly, Yew and Box

Illustrations

xiii

Holly, Yew and Box

A number of the above illustrations have been reproduced by the kindness of the Editor of " The Gardener's Chronicle."

THE HOLLY

HOLLY, YEW & BOX

I

THE HOLLY FAMILY, GENERAL DESCRIPTION

THE genus Ilex, to which the group of trees and shrubs popularly known as Hollies belongs, is included in the order Ilicineæ, and comprises a very large number of species which are as varied in character as they are widely distributed.

Some species, our "Common Holly" for example, form, under favourable circumstances, trees of moderate dimensions, others grow into large, dense bushes, another set is characterised by a looser and more free habit, whilst in the case of another group growth rarely exceeds a few feet in height. The leaves, which are alternate and attended by very minute stipules, also show much variation, for, in addition to some being deciduous and others evergreen, the size, general outline and spininess of the different species varies to a considerable extent. A glance at some of the hardy species is sufficient to illustrate this, for a great difference exists between the extremely spiny leaves of young plants of I. Aqui-

Holly, Yew and Box

folium; the curious five or seven spined leaves
of I. cornuta; the tiny, crenate leaves of
I. crenata; the large, ornamental foliage of I.
latifolia; the long, narrow leaves of I. dipyrena;
the spineless foliage of I. integra, and so on.
Neither is this difference in form, shape and spinyness noticeable between species only, for varieties
of some species show quite as much variation as
do the typical species above mentioned.

The flowers do not exhibit any great difference
in the various species. They are borne from the
leaf axils, are white or cream in colour, usually
fragrant, and may be monœcious, diœcious, or
hermaphrodite. The flowering period is from
April to June, though it is not unusual for a very
light, second crop of bloom to be produced during
July or even later.

The fruits are more or less globose, often
bright red in colour, though sometimes deep red,
purple, black or yellow, and they usually contain
three or four triangular, hard coated, deeply
furrowed seeds. The normal number of seeds in
most of the evergreen Hollies is four in each
fruit, though in one or two species this number
is reduced to from one to three. In the deciduous,
or Prinos set, six seeds are usually found in each
fruit. Although the normal number is four in
the " Common Holly," it not unfrequently happens
that some are undeveloped, whilst many of those
that appear fully matured are unfertile. On

I. ILEX DIPYRENA, 2. I. DIPYRENA ELLIPTICA, 3. I. CORNUTA, 4. I. INSIGNIS, 5. I. OPACA, 6. I. CASSINE, 7. I. GLABRA

All much reduced

General Description

isolated trees, removed twenty or thirty yards from pollen-bearing specimens, it is not an uncommon thing to find from twenty-five to sixty per cent of the seeds barren. In most cases Hollies have to depend on wind or insect agency for pollination, for, though occasionally, perfect stamens bearing good pollen are found on trees bearing principally female flowers, it usually happens that trees which produce fruit, rarely produce perfect stamens ; in such cases the filaments are often of normal size whilst the anthers are undeveloped. On the other hand, trees which produce an abundance of pollen rarely develop female organs in a satisfactory manner. That pollen is occasionally borne by flowers on female trees, and fruits are produced on trees which usually bear male flowers only, is quite true, and in these cases single flowers as a rule bear fully developed male and female organs, the few flowers borne in July and later being more prone to this than the blossoms borne at the normal time. The fact that isolated trees often bear abundant crops of fruit has given rise to the idea that perfect flowers are borne in abundance by some trees : this idea, however, is open to question, for, after careful observation, I have rarely found good pollen on such trees and have found a large number of unfertile seeds, which points to the fact that the flowers have to depend on wind or insects to convey pollen from other trees.

Holly, Yew and Box

The fruits usually ripen in September, and hang on the trees until spring or even later unless attacked by birds.

A considerable difference of opinion has existed on the part of botanists, not only in the creation of species but also in generic title. From the *Index Kewensis* we find that the following generic names have been used at one time or another for species all of which are correctly included in the genus Ilex.

Ageria.	Macoucoua.
Aquifolium.	Othera.
Arinemia.	Paltoria.
Braxylis.	Pileostegia.
Cassine.	Prinodia.
Chomelia.	Prinos.
Ennepta.	Pseudehretia.
Hexotria.	Synstima.
Labatia.	Winterlia.
Leucodermis.	

Of this number the two that concern us most are Othera and Prinos, the former being still occasionally used in commercial establishments for the Japanese I. integra, whilst the latter is associated with certain deciduous species of N. American and Japanese origin.

When such a difference of opinion has existed over the generic name it is not surprising to find that numerous cases of species bearing a multi-

General Description

plicity of names occur, and whilst the number of distinct species recorded in the *Index Kewensis* is 167, the synonyms total 138.

The distribution of the genus is very wide, species being found in Europe, the West Indies, Malaya, Australia, Polynesia, Himalaya, China, Japan, Formosa, N. America, Eastern tropical S. America, N. Africa, and other places. The headquarters of the genus is S. America, and in Brazil alone sixty distinct species have been found. China, Japan and Hong Kong together claim forty described species, whilst it is more than probable that others will be discovered in these regions in the near future, introductions of recent years having added several to the list.

The great variation existing between the varieties of some species has already been noted, and this variation is most pronounced in the " Common Holly " (I. Aquifolium). An idea of the variability of this tree can be gleaned from the fact that upwards of 140 forms have been named, quite 100 being distinct. Even on the same tree different leaves often present totally distinct aspects, whole branches sometimes being affected, whilst at other times isolated, malformed leaves only occur amongst perfect ones. Amongst a batch of seedlings it is no uncommon thing to find great variation in size, form and spinyness of leaf, as well as a difference in habit, whilst on a mature tree it is a

7

common thing to find many of the leaves partially or wholly spineless, especially on the upper branches.

This peculiarity is not confined to the British species, for the same thing occurs amongst some exotic Hollies, notably the N. America I. opaca, and the Chinese I. cornuta, herbarium specimens from mature trees of both these species showing almost, if not quite, spineless leaves, whilst on young trees the leaves are always spiny.

Although the genus is such a large one, comparatively few species are of value for decorative garden work. These are of course the hardier ones, for, although some of the tropical species form ornamental trees in their native places they are of no value for indoor work in this country.

The following is a list of the hardiest species at present in cultivation or likely to be in the near future. Others, known only from herbarium specimens and descriptions, will doubtless be introduced ere long, and if they prove hardy will be of decorative value. Those marked with an asterisk should only be planted in the warmer parts of the country.

European.
Aquifolium.

Canary Island, Madeira, etc.
*Perado, platyphylla.

LEAVES TAKEN FROM A SINGLE SPECIMEN OF COMMON HOLLY,
SHOWING DIFFERENCE IN SIZE, OUTLINE AND SPINYNESS
Much reduced

General Description

China.

corallina, cornuta, Fargesii, Pernyi.

China and Japan.

pedunculosa.

Japan.

crenata, integra, latifolia, macropoda, rugosa,
Sieboldi, Sugeroki.

Himalaya.

dipyrena, insignis.*

N. America.

ambigua, Amelanchier, Cassine, Dahoon, decidua,
glabra, lævigata, opaca, verticillata.

II

PROPAGATION AND GENERAL CULTIVATION OF HOLLIES

Propagation

THE propagation of Hollies is usually effected by one of four ways, *i.e.* by seeds, by cuttings, by budding, or by grafting. To these four might be added layering, for, although not generally adopted, it is quite possible to obtain plants from layered branches.

Seeds are used for the propagation of the "Common Holly" and for some of the exotic species, the other methods being resorted to in the case of the varieties of the "Common Holly" and for species of which seeds cannot be readily obtained. Holly seeds, as a rule, take a long time to germinate, two and sometimes three years elapsing between the sowing of the seeds and the appearance of the seedlings. When raising I. Aquifolium in quantity, seeds are collected as soon as ripe and mixed with two or three times their own bulk of sand, the whole being thrown into a heap and left for twelve months exposed to

Propagation and General Cultivation

the changes of the weather. At the end of this time the sand and seeds are sown together, thinly, in beds 4 feet wide, with paths 12 to 18 inches wide between them for cleaning purposes. After the seedlings appear they are left undisturbed for two years, when they are taken up, graded into sizes, have long, straggling roots trimmed back, and planted in rows in nursery quarters. In this position they are allowed to remain for two years, when they are again transplanted, subsequent transplantings taking place biennially as long as they remain in the nursery. Seeds of rare species should be sown in well-drained pots or pans in a compost made up of equal parts of good, fibrous loam, peat, and sand. The pots must be plunged in ashes, or other suitable material, out-of-doors, fully exposed to climatic changes until the second spring from the time of sowing, when they should be transferred to a warm house, a change which will facilitate germination. As soon as large enough to handle, the seedlings should be pricked off singly into small pots, or be transferred to a prepared bed in a cold frame, the latter being the better method of the two. When large enough to take care of themselves, they may be placed in the open ground.

Cuttings should be made from half-ripe wood of the current season's growth, July and August being a good time for their preparation. They are usually made from 4 to 5 inches long and are most satisfactory when taken with a slight heel of old wood. Very strong, sappy wood should be avoided, that of a thinner and sturdier character being desirable. It is necessary to insert them firmly in light, sandy soil, either in pots, in a bed in a close cold frame, or under a handlight out-of-doors. The pots may either be plunged in a warm propagating case or be stood in a cold frame. Roots are formed slowly and no disturbance of the cuttings should be permitted for at least six months. When rooted and beginning to grow, they may be planted out in a bed in a cold frame or be placed in a sheltered nursery border. Most of the varieties of I. Aquifolium can be increased in this way, as also can such species as I. crenata, I. cornuta, I. dipyrena, etc.

Budding and grafting are practised in the case of the varieties of the "Common Holly." The former operation is performed in summer and the latter in spring. Young plants of the type are used for stocks, and saleable specimens are obtained in a much shorter period than when propagation is effected by means of cuttings. Pendulous forms are usually grafted or budded on stems 6 or 8 feet high, whilst variegated varieties are also grafted on tall stems to form round headed specimens. With grafted plants, care has always to be taken that suckers do not grow from the stock to injure the scion.

Propagation and General Cultivation

Soil

Hollies are not by any means fastidious subjects regarding soil, as they thrive in almost any sort that shrubs can be expected to grow in. The height of perfection is arrived at in that of a well-drained, rich, loamy nature. It is, however, no uncommon thing to find good specimens on both sandy and clayey ground, whilst they grow luxuriantly in soil of a peaty character, as well as in that containing an abundance of lime. In the Woking district of Surrey, where much of the land is eminently suitable for Rhododendron culture, Hollies are remarkably fine both in growth and colour, while the same may be said of districts where it is impossible to grow Rhododendrons through the prevalence of lime in the soil. Water-logged ground is not suitable for Hollies, and in land naturally wet but fairly well drained it is not advisable to plant any but the very commonest, as rank, vigorous shoots are often made which do not ripen well. On a site where a brick building has been demolished, Hollies are often found flourishing in fine form, the roots running riot among the old mortar and bits of brick left in the soil.

Planting

More care has to be exercised in the planting of Hollies than is necessary with some trees and

13

shrubs. In every instance the ground should be well worked, and if very poor, good, loamy soil ought to be introduced in order to give the plants a good start. In the case of very heavy land it is advisable to add good gritty sand during the digging or trenching. Throughout the nursery period, as has been previously stated, the stock should be transplanted every second year; and even large specimens, that are intended for some other position eventually, are in better condition for transplanting if dug round every two or three years and strong roots pruned back to a suitable distance from the stem. As a rule it is advisable to move the plants with a quantity of soil attached to the roots, and with specimens of any great size it may be said to be absolutely necessary; for, although now and then, a large specimen will grow that has been removed without soil, the chances are greatly against it.

The correct time to transplant Hollies with the minimum amount of soil, is either very early in autumn, say the last week in August and through September, or in late spring, the latter end of April and May. At either of these times the roots are very active and begin to work into the new soil quickly, whereas if transplanting is done in late autumn, winter, or very early spring, the roots lie dormant for a long while and often rot instead of grow, consequently no food material is available to keep the plant going. In

Propagation and General Cultivation

the event of specimens being transplanted with large masses of earth, the time of year is not so important, in fact, the work may be done at almost any period, as the roots are not disturbed to any serious extent. Should considerable root disturbance take place at the time of planting, it is advisable to cut away some of the branches, so that by reducing the leaf surface, the bad effect caused by injury to the feeding roots is to some extent counter-balanced, through there being a reduced leaf surface.

Roots that are injured in any way during planting operations should be carefully cut back beyond the injured places. A good watering is usually necessary as soon as the planting is finished, and in the event of dry weather ensuing, repeated applications of water will be required. With valuable specimens and hedges it is even advisable to syringe over-head two or three times a day, and provide some sort of shading material for a month or two after transplanting, should the weather prove very hot and dry.

Although fresh dung near the roots is not appreciated by Hollies, surfacing the ground with a mixture of well rotted manure and leaves during dry weather will be found beneficial alike to newly planted and established specimens. It is also advisable to hoe the surface of the ground occasionally about newly planted Hollies, particularly in the case of hedges in heavy ground.

Holly, Yew and Box

Pruning

Pruning is usually confined to Hollies used for ornamental purposes. Those growing in woods require no other attention than keeping the leaders clear, except when grown for some special purpose, such as whip handles or walking sticks. The pruning of garden specimens is usually done in one of two ways. The first method is applicable to trees allowed to grow in a fairly natural manner. In this case it consists of keeping the leaders clear, removing growths that are reverting from the typical form of any particular variety, reducing parts that are developing out of all proportion to other parts, and the removal of dead wood and branches growing into the ground. This can be done by thinning out branches so as to leave the tree or bush in as natural a manner as possible. The second method is a more barbarous one, and one that is not to be generally commended. The trees are clipped hard back every year, in a similar manner to a hedge, so as to form pyramids, cones, globes or other patterns, which look as if they had been turned out of moulds. Trees or bushes clipped in this way can only be used in very formal parts of the garden, and even then it is very questionable whether they can be called ornamental. Young plants that have got into a stunted state can be improved by being cut well down to induce a

GROUP OF VARIETIES OF COMMON HOLLY

Propagation and General Cultivation

strong shoot to appear, and even in the event of old trees or hedges that have become weak at the bottom, a good cutting back will often result in the formation of strong young shoots. Specimens that have lost their leads can be renovated by tying up a central branch.

Feeding

Specimens growing in poor ground that are not acting in a satisfactory manner can be improved by removing some of the soil from about the roots and replacing it with rich loam. An occasional top-dressing of well-rotted manure may be given, and an application twice a year, April and August, of cow-manure water.

Enemies

Hollies are comparatively free from insect attacks. Occasionally, the young shoots and leaves are attacked by a black aphis which can be destroyed by spraying the affected plants with a strong solution of soft soap or tobacco water. A species of scale called Aspidiotus britannicus attacks leaves and branches, and sometimes causes serious damage. This can be destroyed by spraying affected plants once every ten days during the latter half of March, April, and early May with strong soft soap water, into

Holly, Yew and Box

every four gallons of which ½ a pint of paraffin has been mixed. A fly, commonly known as the " Holly Fly," with the scientific name of Phytomyza Ilicis, attacks the leaves in some parts of the country. The eggs are deposited below the epidermis, and the resulting grubs, which, when mature, are about ¼ of an inch long, feed on the leaf, with the result that small patches die and turn to a light brown colour. If the attack is not very bad, all the affected leaves should be picked off and burnt. If attacks are very bad, the trees should be sprayed with the paraffin and soft soap mixture once a week during April, May, and June, the period when the flies are active.

Mice, rabbits and hares sometimes injure plants by nibbling the bark round the trunks and lower branches, and local conditions will have to be considered when dealing with these animals.

III

THE USES OF THE HOLLIES

THE majority of the cultivated Hollies are grown solely on account of their decorative value, and their usefulness in this direction quite overshadows other uses to which some of the species can be put. As decorative plants they may be used in a variety of ways, such as isolated lawn specimens, bold groups on lawns, plantation work, or undergrowth in moderately thin woods. As a hedge plant the "Common Holly" has few equals for British gardens, whilst in part of the United States the same can be said of the "American Holly" (I. opaca).

To the "Common Holly" several qualities are attributed other than purely decorative ones, and a glance at these may not be out of place. In *Gray's British Plants* reference is made to the berries of the "Common Holly" being used in cases of colic, whilst the following extract bearing on the medicinal qualities is taken from the *Treasury of Botany*. "The leaves are stated on good authority to be equal to Peruvian bark in the cure of intermittent fevers. The

Holly, Yew and Box

root and bark are said to be deobstruent, expectorant and diuretic, agreeably to which *Haller* recommends the juice of the leaves in jaundice. The berries are purgative and emetic, six or eight being sufficient, it is said, to produce the latter effect." The same work goes on to say, "it has been stated recently by M. J. Pierre, that the young stems are gathered in Morbihan by the peasants, and made use of as a cattle food from the end of November to April with great success. The stems are dried, and having been bruised are given as food to cows three times a day. They are found to be very wholesome and very productive of good milk, and the butter made from it is excellent."

The timber, which sometimes grows to a considerable size, is beautifully white, and very tough and hard. It is used to some extent for turning, in the manufacture of mathematical instruments, and by cabinet-makers for inlaying purposes. Formerly it was sought after for making pulley-blocks for ships, and is sometimes still used for that purpose. In building construction the wood was formerly used for beams of houses in positions where they would enter chimneys, as the wood does not catch fire easily. In the early part of the last century the knots and burrs, which are sometimes found on the trunk, were used for the making of snuff boxes. Young, straight, quickly grown shoots are used to some

The Uses of the Hollies

considerable extent for the making of walking sticks and whip handles, while the rough timber forms excellent mallets. In some instances the wood is ebonized and substituted for ebony.

In former years, when the snaring of birds with birdlime was prevalent, the "Common Holly" was in great demand, for the principal source of birdlime was its mucilaginous bark, and *Evelyn* in his *Silva* gives a full account of its preparation.

This account is as follows :—"Peel a good quantity of the bark of the young shoots about mid-summer ; fill a vessel with it, and put to it spring water, then boil it till the grey and white bark rises from the green, which will require near 12 hours boiling ; then taking it off the fire, separate the barks, the water first being drained off. Then lay the green bark on the earth in some cool vault or cellar, covering it with any sort of green or rank weeds, litter or mats to a good thickness. Thus let it continue near a fortnight, by which time in consequence of fermentation it will have become a perfect mucilage ; then pound it all exceedingly well in a stone mortar, till it be a tough paste, and so very fine that no part of the bark is discernible. This done, wash it accurately well in some running stream of water as long as you perceive the least impurities in it, and so reserve it in some earthen pot to ferment, scumming it as often as anything

Holly, Yew and Box

arises for four or five days, and when no more filth comes to the top, change it into a fresh earthen vessel and prepare it for use thus :— Take what quantity you please of it, and, in an earthen pipkin, add a third of capon's fat, or goose grease, to it, well clarified, or oil of walnuts, which is better ; incorporate these on a gentle fire, continually stirring it till it be cold, and thus your composition is finished." *Hunter's Evelyn, p.* 268.

At Christmas time a great deal of berried Holly finds its way into the market for house and church decoration, and in some parts of the country a considerable industry has sprung up in the growing and selling of cut Holly.

To I. opaca are credited similar qualities to those of the European plant, whilst I. Cassine, or I. vomitaria as it is often called, is used by the North American Indians as an emetic.

From the leaves of a tropical species from S. America, I. paraguayensis, the "Mate" or "Paraguay Tea" is prepared. This tea is used largely in some parts of S. America in preference to that prepared from the leaves of Camellia theifera.

IV

HOLLIES AS SPECIMEN PLANTS

THE evergreen Hollies are especially adapted for forming specimen plants, in fact the majority of the varieties never look better than when standing alone, or arranged in groups wide enough apart so that no two plants touch. Even when employed in mixed shrubberies, it is advisable to let them stand well out of the surrounding vegetation and to remove other plants from the vicinity as they increase in growth, so that no appearance of crowding will be apparent. As the majority of the Hollies form evenly balanced specimens with very little attention to training, they are subjects that cause comparatively little trouble, whilst they always look bright and vigorous. Their superiority over such other evergreens as the majority of Coniferous trees is very evident in places where the atmosphere is at all impure, for, while the Conifers, as a rule, are painful to behold, and eke out but a lingering existence for a few years, the Hollies usually thrive, form fine plants, and live for several generations.

23

Holly, Yew and Box

Grown as specimens, either isolated or in groups, great care should be taken with any necessary pruning. The greater number are naturally of pyramidal outline and inclined to be a little formal whilst young. If allowed to grow freely and the necessary pruning is done in the manner previously described, so that a loose branch effect is left, the natural formality of habit is not objectionable, but, when as is too often the case, the pruning takes the form of clipping, and trees are made to look like gigantic, green-painted sugar loaves or inflated plum puddings, the effect is absurd and positively cruel. In the case of hedges, clipping has to be done, but what pleasure people can find in practically planing the head of such a fine tree as the Holly passes all comprehension.

For certain styles of gardening we are told that this hard clipping is absolutely essential, if that is so, keep it within gardens of these particular styles and relegate them to the retired list, or keep them here and there as a sort of museum example of what was met with in bygone days.

The last decade or two has certainly done much to banish many objectionable features from gardens, and a freer and more natural style is, generally, more in evidence than was previously the case : there are, however, a few things that need alteration, and one is the hard clipping of beautiful Hollies.

ILEX AQUIFOLIUM CAMELLIÆFOLIA.   IN THE ROYAL GARDENS, KEW

Hollies as Specimen Plants

For the garden proper the rarer species and the best of the varieties of I. Aquifolium should be used as specimens, whilst for the wilder parts the type of the "Common Holly" and the yellow fruited variety are the most desirable.

On open lawns the pendulous Hollies can be used with great effect, the "Common Green Weeping" and "Perry's Weeping" being most often met with. At Kew several fine examples of "Weeping Hollies" are to be found, the largest one standing on a lawn near the Succulent House. This is 15 feet high, 50 feet in circumference, and of uniform outline. A few years ago many large specimen Hollies, both of ordinary and weeping habit, were to be seen in the Necropolis Cemetery at Brookwood.

The following species and varieties form good specimens :—I. Aquifolium and varieties angusti-folia, argentea marginata, argentea medio-picta, argentea pendula, argentea regina, Handsworth New Silver, aurifodina, aurea marginata, aurea medio-picta, aurea regina, ciliata, crispa, donning-tonensis, ferox, ferox argentea, fructu luteo, hands-worthensis, integrifolia, laurifolia, camelliæfolia, myrtifolia, scotica, ovata, Watereriana, and whit-tingtonensis ; I. cornuta, I. dipyrena, I. latifolia, I. opaca, I. platyphylla and varieties, I. Mundyi, I. Wilsoni, I. altaclarensis, I. Hodginsii, etc.

V

THE HOLLIES AS TOWN TREES

THE evergreen Hollies, more particularly the "Common Holly" and its varieties, form an exceptionally useful group for town planting, and the proprietors of private gardens as well as municipal bodies would do well to give them special attention. Unfortunately, municipal bodies are not usually endowed with the collecting spirit where trees and shrubs are concerned, and instead of them setting about the formation of really good collections of these items in the parks under their control, they content themselves with planting large quantities of a few things which are more often than not the most everyday subjects imaginable. Parks planted with a judicious selection of good trees and shrubs would be infinitely more interesting than many are at the present time; the expense would not be great, if a nursery for raising young stock was attached to the parks of each town, and future generations would be benefited by fine examples of rare trees instead of common ones. Every town, in fact, might have a really good

HOLLY "GOLDEN QUEEN"

The Hollies as Town Trees

Arboretum if the work was set about in a methodical manner.

When dealing with Hollies an interesting and scientific collection might be formed in many towns and it would be the means of keeping in cultivation many rare species and varieties which are in danger of becoming lost, few private growers having the space and convenience to keep together large collections. In some of the London parks very good Hollies are to be found, satisfactory examples being also met with in some provincial towns. In too many cases, however, the number of varieties found is very small. About towns or districts of towns with an atmosphere heavily laden with smoke or chemical fumes, where plant life generally leads but a lingering existence, it would of course be inadvisable to attempt to grow a great variety of sorts; dependence in such a case would be better placed on anything that will keep green. There are, however, parks in many towns where Hollies would thrive admirably and a most interesting feature could be produced.

In the Grosvenor Park, Chester, Hollies grow with remarkable freedom, and the nucleus of a collection was formed thirty years or more ago. This has not, unfortunately, been added to, and some fifteen or eighteen sorts are all that are to be seen. The great feature of this park is provided by upwards of 120 large examples of

Holly, Yew and Box

I. Hodginsii. The greater number are planted in the form of avenues, but in the instance of the best avenue they are alternated with Limes which have grown out of all proportion and quite kill the effect of the Hollies.

For suburban gardens the Hollies are to be recommended as they always look fresh, for, from the glossy nature of their leaves, dirt is readily washed away by rain. For smoke-laden districts it is better to select varieties with glossy rather than dull leaves.

ILEX PLATYPHYLLA NIGRESCENS

VI

THE HOLLIES AS HEDGE PLANTS

ALTHOUGH several species of Ilex would be of value for the formation of hedges, the "Common Holly" is so easily obtained, so eminently fitted for the purpose, and so generally esteemed in all countries where it thrives, that it has been unnecessary to try other sorts which it is difficult to procure in suitable quantities. In America, I. opaca, which is to America what I. Aquifolium is to Britain and southern European countries, is used in much the same way as the "Common Holly" is here, and is said to form excellent hedges.

The usefulness of the Holly for forming hedges has been appreciated for a very long period, and quite three centuries ago we find that it was requisitioned for the purpose in British gardens. Even much longer ago than that we find evidences of hedges having been formed of the Holly. In 1838 a correspondent to the *Floricultural Cabinet, p.* 198, in writing about Hollies says, "Columella seems to have recommended the

Holly, Yew and Box

Holly to the Romans as a proper fence for gardens. In his tenth book he says,

" And let such grounds with walls or prickly Hedge
Thick set, surrounded be and well secured,
Not pervious to the cattle nor the thieves."

On October 15th, 1662, *Mr John Evelyn* lectured before the Royal Society on *Forest Trees*, and this lecture was afterwards published in book form entitled *A Silva, or Discourse on Forest Trees*. In this work he dwells at some considerable length upon the beauty and virtues of the Holly for various purposes, giving particular attention to its value as a hedge plant. In one place he says—" Of this might there living pales and enclosures be made, such as the Right Honourable, my Lord Dacres, somewhere in Sussex, has a park almost environed with, able to keep in any game as I am credibly informed ; and cut into square hedges it is impenetrable, and will thrive in hottest and coldest places."

Growing in his own garden was a Holly hedge of which he was inordinately proud, and of this he writes, " Is there under heaven a more glorious and refreshing object of the kind than an impregnable hedge of about 400 feet in length, 9 feet high, and 5 feet in diameter, which I can show in my own ruined garden at Say's Court at any time of the year, glittering with its armed and varnished leaves, the taller standards at orderly distances, blushing with their natural

The Hollies as Hedge Plants

coral. It mocks at the rudest assaults of weather, beasts, or hedge breakers."

On the point of its beautiful appearance, impregnable nature, and value for keeping out undesirables, he speaks with great freedom, and quotes the following verse on behalf of his contentions :—

> "A Hedge of Holly, Thieves that would invade
> Repulses like a growing Palisade
> Whose numerous leaves such Orient Greens invest
> As in deep winter do the spring arrest."

Coming down to more recent times, we find some famous Holly hedges mentioned in *Selby's British Forest Trees*, published in 1842. In the Earl of Haddington's garden at Tynynghame it is stated that "2952 yards of hedges existed, which varied in width from 9 to 13 feet and in height from 10 to 25 feet." At that time many of these hedges were said to be 127 years old. Upon enquiry I learn that 25 years ago they showed signs of deterioration and required vigorous treatment in the way of cutting back, this however was not done, and they have now fallen into a state of general decay. When at their best these hedges were said to be remarkable objects, and it is stated that in order to protect them from cattle, ditches had been made along each side. Other fine hedges are said by *Selby* to have existed at Collington House and Morton, near Edinburgh.

31

Holly, Yew and Box

At the present time, really good hedges of Holly are held in as high estimation as ever, and the owner of a good one is usually every bit as proud of it as Evelyn was, whilst it excites the envy of all his associates. In the neighbourhood of Bagshot a fine hedge exists which I am informed exceeds 30 feet in height, a photograph of this is given in the third edition of *Robinson's English Flower Garden*. At Kew a fine Holly hedge surrounds the Shrub Nursery in the Arboretum : this is 315 yards long, and the greater part is 9 feet high and 4 feet wide ; one portion has, however, been allowed to assume greater proportions and measures 12 feet in height and 7 feet in width.

When planting Holly hedges it is necessary to work the ground well to a depth of 2 feet, more especially is this the case if the land is naturally heavy. Plants from 1 to 5 feet high may be obtained, but it is not desirable, except for very special purposes, to have plants much higher than 5 feet, as after that they become difficult to transplant with safety. The position of the hedge is of no great importance, as Hollies thrive in partial shade and full sun, and on a variety of soils. With regard to soil Evelyn speaks of his famous hedge as follows :—" And this rare hedge, the boast of my Villa, was planted upon a burning gravel exposed to the meridian sun." As previously stated, the time of planting may be

The Hollies as Hedge Plants

either very early autumn or late spring. The plants selected should show signs of a vigorous constitution, have good leads, and be well furnished with branches to within a few inches of the ground. The distance apart to place the plants will depend entirely on their size, anything from a foot or 15 inches to 2½ feet being desirable. If the soil has been removed from the roots for purposes of transit it will be advisable to prune the branches a little to counterbalance the ill effects of root disturbance. Care should be taken to work the soil well in among the roots, and a good watering should be given as soon as the plants are in position. If the roots seem to be at all dry they should be watered before being placed in the ground. To keep the bottoms well clothed it is advisable to check the upward tendency so as to throw strength into the lower branches.

Some people prefer to plant a mixture of Holly and White Thorn about four or five of the latter to one of Holly. This makes a strong fence and is cheaper than planting all Holly. Evelyn states that his hedge was first planted in this way. In an old book I have come across an account of another way of planting a Holly hedge. This advises laying well rooted sets down and earthing them over, after which it is stated that they will break well and quickly form a good hedge.

To keep a hedge in good order it is necessary

Holly, Yew and Box

to keep the sides and top clipped back at least once a year. This work may be done either in spring or autumn, April being a good time, as young growth then quickly appears to hide mutilated leaves. Some old writers recommend cutting hedges back with a knife to save the disfigurement of the leaves; this of course is impracticable where large hedges are concerned. If the annual cutting back is persisted in, a hedge soon becomes very dense, and it is almost impossible to see into it. One can very easily understand the redoubtable Wallace being quite safe on the occasion, when over six centuries ago he is stated to have hidden from his enemies in a hedge "Off great Hollyns that grew baith heych and greyn." (See *Johnston's Botany of the Eastern Borders.*)

In some parts the practice still prevails, as it did in Evelyn's time, of allowing standards to grow out of and above hedges, and sometimes variegated foliaged sorts are employed, alternated with green, for the purpose. In some positions this arrangement is very effective, but it is not desirable in all cases.

For uncommon hedges where money is no object the stronger growing gold and silver varieties might be employed, whilst for an informal fence in a prominent position, the low growing, but elegant, tiny leaved I. crenata would be a desirable subject.

The Hollies as Hedge Plants

The cost of "Common Hollies" for hedges varies somewhat in different parts of the country, but may be averaged as follows :—1 to 1½ feet high, 35s. a hundred; 1½ to 2 feet high, 55s. a hundred.

VII

I. AQUIFOLIUM

History, Description, etc.

THIS is undoubtedly the oldest, best known and most useful of all the species of Ilex. From old writers we learn that it was a favourite tree and largely used in connection with various festivals in the time of the Romans, whilst mention is made of it in the writings of our earliest horticulturists.

Previous to *Linnæus* adopting the name of Ilex for the genus, this plant was called both Agrifolium and Aquifolium, the latter name being eventually accepted by *Linnæus* to distinguish the species. *Loudon* says in his *Arboretum et Fruticetum Britannicum*, that "Theophrastus and other Greek authors named the Holly Agria; that is, wild or of the fields; and the Romans formed from this the word Agrifolium; and called it also Aquifolium, from acutum, sharp, and folium, a leaf."

The common name of Holly is also of great antiquity. The reason for the name being given is open to conjecture, the most plausible one

GROUP OF COMMON HOLLIES

I. Aquifolium: History, etc.

being that it is a corruption of Holy, as in some old works we find it called the Holy-tree, probably on account of its being so deeply associated with the festival of Christmas and other religious observances. In Germany it bears the name of Christdorn, and a legend is common in that country that leaves of the Holly were employed to form the "crown of thorns" for the Saviour previous to the crucifixion.

In addition to the common name of Holly, it is met with in some places under the names of Holy, Hulver, and Holm; names which have been perpetuated by the christening of villages and houses after them, such as Holly Springs, Holly Mount, Holly Fort, Hollywood, Holmwood, Holmsville, Holytown, Holycross, Hulverwood, etc.

I. Aquifolium is widely distributed through parts of central and southern Europe, and is a common plant in the British Isles, particularly in England and Scotland, where it often assumes large proportions. It also extends to Asia and is found as far east as Central China; a variety known as I. A. chinensis being found in the Celestial Empire. In the Balearic Islands a distinct Holly is found which appears to be a connecting link between I. Aquifolium and species common to N. Africa and the Azores.

In habit it is met with as a moderate sized

Holly, Yew and Box

bush and also in the form of a tree anything from 20 to 80 feet in height, with a trunk several feet in circumference. Growing in the open it assumes the form of a more or less pyramidal bush, clothed with branches from the ground upwards. Planted in a position where it is crowded by other trees it is drawn up, loses its lower branches, and when mature forms a somewhat spreading head.

The evergreen leaves are very dark in colour, alternate, stipulate (the stipules being brown and very minute), more or less oval, $2\frac{1}{2}$ to 5 inches in length and $\frac{3}{4}$ to 2 inches wide, coriaceous in texture, with wavy and intensely spiny margins when young, the spines being fewer in number and sometimes altogether absent on old specimens. The flowers, which are white and fragrant, are borne in axillary clusters during May and early June. They vary in character on different plants and also occasionally on the same plant, some being staminate only, others pistillate, and others again hermaphrodite. The fruits are round, about $\frac{1}{4}$ of an inch in diameter, bright red when ripe, and contain from one to four triangular seeds. They hang on the trees for several months if undisturbed by unnatural agencies, and have been known to remain until a second year's fruit has been perfected.

I. Aquifolium : History, etc.

Age

The "Common Holly" is naturally a long lived tree. The exact, or even approximate age to which it will live under favourable circumstances is not known, but there is no doubt of trees living from 250 to 300 years. *Loudon* gives a quotation from *Pliny* bearing on the age of Hollies as follows :—"Tiburtus built the city of Tibur near three Holly-trees, over which he had observed the flight of birds that pointed out the spot whereon the Gods had fixed for its erection, and that these trees were standing in his own time and must therefore be upwards of 1200 years old." He also tells us that "there was a Holly-tree then growing near the Vatican in Rome on which was fixed a brass plate with an inscription engraved in Tuscan letters, and that this tree was older than Rome itself, which must have been more than 800 years." *Book XVI. Chap.* 44.

Dimensions

In the description of one of these trees *Pliny* says, "the trunk measured 35 feet in circumference, and that it sent out ten branches of such magnitude that each might pass for a tree, and that the single tree resembled a small wood."

Loudon says that the largest tree in England

Holly, Yew and Box

in his day grew at Claremont in Surrey : it was 80
feet high, with a head 25 feet in diameter and a
trunk with a diameter of 2 feet 2 inches. The
largest tree in England that I have been able to
discover is growing at Mount Edgcumbe. This
is 70 feet high with a clear trunk of 30 feet,
which is 6 feet in girth at 3 feet above the ground,
and a branch-spread of 42 feet.

At Kew the largest tree, now unfortunately
in a dying condition, is 50 feet high with a girth
of 5 feet 8 inches at 3 feet above the ground and
7 feet 9 inches near the ground. A healthy
specimen with a double trunk near the south end
of the rockery is 55 feet high with a trunk girth
of 4 feet 10 inches at 3 feet above the ground.

Several fine specimens are reported from
Scotland, notably at Tynynghame, the seat of the
Earl of Haddington, where one which in 1812
girthed 5 feet 5 inches at 5 feet above the ground,
measured in November 1906, 6 feet 7 inches at
a similar height. Other trees on the same estate
with tall, clear stems girth between 5½ and 6 feet.
At Carnsalloch, in Dumfries, there is a tree 35
feet high with a girth of 6¼ feet.

The Encyclopædia Britannica records a tree
growing on Bleak Hill, Shropshire, with a girth
of 14 feet at some distance above the ground.

Selby, in his *Forest Trees, pp.* 33-40, mentions
a historic tree at Floors Castle, Roxburghshire,
which marked the place where James II. was

I. Aquifolium : History, etc.

killed during the siege of Roxburgh Castle. This tree, I am informed, died about 30 years ago, and has been replaced by a young specimen.

Cole in his *Paradise of Plants* refers to a large Holly-tree which came under his observation as follows :—" I knew a tree of this kind that grew in an orchard, and the owner cut it down and caused it to be sawn into boards and made himself thereof a coffin, and, if I mistake not, left enough to make his wife one also. Both the parties were very corpulent, and therefore you may imagine the tree could not be small."

Distribution in the British Isles

Formerly, Hollies were more abundant in woods both in England and Scotland than they are now, and we are informed in *Johnston's Botany of the Eastern Borders*, 1853, that several remains of natural woods were to be found at Detchant, near Belford, in Northumberland, many trees being of very large size, but that they were being cut down and the valuable timber used by herring curers. At Twizell House large trees of ancient growth are also recorded. *Loudon* quotes from *Lauder's Gilpin, I. p.* 194, that "the Holly is found in great abundance on the banks of the river Findhorn in Aberdeenshire, and the trees grow to a very great size. So plentiful were they in the forest of Tarnwara on its left bank, that

Holly, Yew and Box

for many years the castle of Tarnwara was supplied with no other fuel than billets of Holly. and yet the trees are still so numerous that, in going through the woods in 1834, no one would suppose that any such destruction had been committed."

In many parts of England Hollies are still found in quantity in a more or less wild state, the New Forest being worthy of special mention.

Loudon states that the Holly is not so common in Ireland as it is in England and Scotland, but that large ones are to be found about Killarney, and mentions one on Innisfallen Island with a trunk 15 feet in circumference. He also mentions a variegated Silver Holly at Ballygannon 28 feet high with a trunk 5 feet in circumference.

Medicinal and other Properties

Although the Holly possesses some medicinal qualities, and doctors and herbalists of two or three centuries ago spoke in high terms of the value of the fruits and decoctions of the bark and leaves for various complaints, I am informed that modern practitioners make absolutely no use of it in medicines.

Some of the virtues attributed to it by old writers are truly wonderful. For instance *Parkinson*, in his *Theatrum Botanicum, pp.* 1486-7, quotes as follows : — " Matthiolus saith that a

I. Aquifolium: History, etc.

decoction of roots of the Holly, but the bark of the root is the most powerful, fomented on places out of joint, doeth help them much and also helps to consolidate broken bones."

A writer in *Hardwicke's Science Gossip* in referring to the medicinal properties says:—"Later on the bark and leaves were used in fomentations, and the dried and not dried berries were reputed to possess very opposite qualities when swallowed. In my young days, when I suffered from chilblains, I was told that if I would only submit to have them whipped with freshly gathered Holly-leaves till the blood flowed, they would soon heal and never again appear. I had not the courage to try this remedy, but I believe it is still used in some country places."

This cure for chilblains is still recommended in villages in Cheshire.

On the virtues of the seeds taken in doses of ten or twelve, in cases of constipation, *Culpepper*, *Gerard*, *Parkinson*, and *Johnson*, all wax eloquent, whilst *Johnson*, who published a *Herbal* in 1633, warns everyone against taking birdlime, made from Holly, inwardly, and goes on in language more forcible than polite to describe the evil effects produced on persons who should be unwise enough to take a dose.

Strange to say, at a later date one writer recommends a decoction of the bark as a cure for a cough, whilst in *Sowerby's English Botany, II.*

Holly, Yew and Box

p. 221, it is stated that "Dr Rousseau of Paris, who published a paper in the *Transactions of the Medico-Botanical Society of London*, recommends a decoction of Holly leaves and bark, as well as a new principle extracted therefrom and called ilicine, as equal to and sometimes better than quinine."

The uses of the timber have been previously referred to, together with other economic properties of the tree.

Variation in the Sex of Flowers

The difference of sex in the flowers of the Holly has at one time or another attracted considerable attention. *Thomas Martyn, B.D., F.R.S., Regius Professor of Botany* at the *University of Cambridge*, upwards of a century ago edited an edition of *Philip Miller's Dictionary of Plants* in 1797, and in it he claims that his father first noticed the difference in sex of Holly flowers, for he says, "the difference in sex was first noticed by my father in his garden at Stretham in Surrey; he had many of these trees which before he had possession of the place were shorn into round heads; he emancipated them from their slavery, pruned them and trained up their leading shoots; seeming glad to be released from their shackles, they quickly shot up into goodly trees and soon rewarded him with this discovery

44

I. Aquifolium : History, etc.

regarding their flowers, which he communicated to the Royal Society and is printed in their transactions." Although this appears to be the first scientific notice of the phenomenon, it seems quite likely that the fact of male and female Hollies existing was previously known to the lay mind, for the terms "He and She Hollies" are very old.

VIII

I. AQUIFOLIUM—*Continued*

Legends, Superstitions, etc.

WITH a plant that has been in general use for so many centuries, it might naturally be supposed that a great many legends and superstitions would centre round it, and such is the case, numerous ones having originated through its use for Christmas decorations. When it was first used for this purpose it is impossible to say, but, anterior to the Christian era it appears to have been made use of in the celebration of idolatrous festivals, more particularly the festival of the Saturnalia, a feast given over to wanton excesses of all descriptions, at which time all old books agree that it was used in large quantities. The early Christians, we are informed (see *Selby's British Trees* and other works), adopted the use of the Holly in the celebration of Christmas, so that they should not be conspicuous amongst their countrymen who were celebrating the great Saturnalian feast. Other authors ascribe its use to a probable relic of Druidism. In reference to

I. Aquifolium : Legends, etc.

this, *Dr Chandler* in his *Travels in Greece* says, "houses were decked with them (Holly branches), that the sylvan spirits might repair to them unnipped by frosts and cold winds, until a milder season had renewed the foliage of their darling abodes."

There is an English superstition which probably had its origin in much the same manner as the foregoing. It says that "Holly was brought in so that the fays might hang in each leaf and cling on each bough during Christmas time when spirits had no power" (see *Plant Lore, Legends and Lyrics*, by *Richard Folkard, Jun.*). In the same work the following statement is made. "In commemoration of the infant Saviour having laid on a manger, it is customary, in some parts of Italy, to deck mangers at Christmas time with Moss, Sow Thistle, Cypress, and prickly Holly."

The origin of the use of Holly for Christmas decorations in our own country is difficult to trace, though quite likely it was a custom brought by the Romans. Conclusive evidence however exists to show that it was popular several centuries ago under the various names of Holm, Hulver, Holy and Holly. *Loudon* in his *Arboretum et Fruticetum, Vol. III. p.* 512, says, "the first record of its use for Christmas decorations was in the time of Henry VI.," when the following quaint carol was composed

47

Holly, Yew and Box

and is now preserved in the *Harleian MS. No.* 5396 :—

> " Nay, Ivy, nay, it shall not be, I wys ;
> Let Holy hafe the maystry, as the manner ys.
> Holy stond in the Halle, fayre to behold ;
> Ivy stond without the dore ; she ys full sore cold.
>
> Holy and hys mery men they dawnsyn and they syng,
> Ivy and hur maydenys they wepyn and they wryng.
> Ivy hath a lybe, she laghtit with the cold,
> So wot they all hafe that wyth Ivy hold.
>
> Holy hath berys as red as any Rose,
> They foster the hunters, kepe him from the doo.
> Ivy hath berys as black as any slo ;
> There com the oule and ete hym as she goo.
>
> Holy hath byrdys, aful fayre flok,
> The Nyghtyngale, the Poppyngy, the gayntul Lavyrok.
> Good Ivy ! what byrdys art thou !
> Non but the Howlet that ' How ! How ! ' "

In some parts of the country, people are very particular to put Holly up for Christmas decorations on a certain day and take it down on a certain day. In other places it is considered to be very unlucky to take Holly into a house before Christmas Eve, and in other districts it is said to be decidedly unfortunate for an invalid if anyone takes a branch of Holly into a sick room, the patient being almost sure to have a serious relapse or possibly die. This superstition, I am informed, still prevails in some parts of Middlesex.

48

I. Aquifolium : Legends, etc.

As it is considered unlucky to take Holly into a house before Christmas Eve, so it is also said to be unlucky if it is not taken down before Candlemas Eve, and as a punishment to the maidens who have neglected the work, goblins will appear and frighten them.

In connection with this superstition the following verse by *Herrick*, culled from the pages of *Plant Lore, p.* 377, is presented :—

> "Down with the Holly and Ivy all
> Wherewith ye deck the Christmas Hall,
> So that the superstitious find
> No one least branch there left behind ;
> For look how many leaves there be
> Neglected there—maids 'tend to me—
> So many goblins ye shall see."

A common idea prevailed in some country places a few years ago that dire disaster would attend the occupants of a house who were unwise enough to take their Holly down before Shrove Tuesday, at which time it must be burnt on the same fire as that on which pancakes were fried.

In some out-of-the-way parts of Kent a custom was in vogue some years ago for the girls of various villages to make guys of Holly branches to burn on Shrove Tuesday, the lads retaliating with guys of Ivy.

According to the *Encyclopædia Britannica*, a superstition prevails in Worcestershire and Herefordshire to the effect that Holly that has

Holly, Yew and Box

been used for church decoration is highly valuable, as the keeping of a berried sprig ensures the owner a lucky year.

The same work informs us that in Derbyshire the opinion prevails that "according as to whether smooth or rough leaved Holly is taken into a house at Christmas, so will the wife or husband be master for the year."

The superstitious legends pertaining to the Holly are not confined to its use at Christmas time, for many have been recorded relating to quite different affairs. Young men and maidens have not been forgotten, for the Holly is credited with having the power, if used in the proper manner, of giving love-sick girls and youths glimpses of their future partners. For instance, in *Johnston's Botany of the Eastern Borders* the following tale, culled from the *Border Tale Book, Vol. VIII. p.* 245, is related :—

" In the north of Northumberland the Holly is divided into two kinds, the He and the She. The former is distinguished by having prickly leaves, while in the latter they are unarmed or nearly so. When gathered in the proper manner, and at the fit hour, the She-Holly engenders dreams concerning that all absorbing subject a husband or wife. To ensure success the leaves must be pulled upon a Friday night at midnight, by parties who, from their setting out until next day at dawn, must preserve unbroken silence.

I. Aquifolium : Legends, etc.

Nine leaves are to be collected in a three cornered handkerchief, tied up with nine knots and then put under the pillow. A dream worthy of credit is the result."

In *Plant Lore* another method is given of obtaining a view of a young lady's future husband, but unfortunately her curiosity can very rarely be gratified, for the spell is only credited with being of use on four days of the year; these are All Hallowe'en, Christmas Eve, New Year's Eve, and Midsummer Eve. The story goes that "a maiden must place three pails of water on her bedroom floor, then pin three leaves of green Holly to her nightdress over her heart, and retire to bed. She will be aroused from her first sleep by three terrible yells, followed by three hoarse laughs, after which the form of her future husband will appear. If he is deeply attached to her, he will change the position of the water pails; if not, he will glide from the room without touching them." It is not difficult to imagine the three yells being true, if the young lady had selected nice spiny leaves and was at all restless.

In an old number of *Hardwicke's Science Gossip* the following paragraphs appear :—

"Great interest attaches to some Holly-trees. In Argyllshire there is a prophecy that when a particular Holly-tree near Inverary ceases to exist, and when certain other things shall happen (some of which have already come to pass), then

Holly, Yew and Box

shall all the Argyll Campbells be destroyed, excepting so many as shall escape on a crooked and lame white horse; and we learn from *Notes and Queries* that, in 1861, 'the roots were exposed and loosened by the tide, and that the grandfather of the present Duke of Argyll insisted on an awkward bend being made in the line of public road to avoid the necessity of cutting it down.'

"Near Dilston, in Northumberland, there is a thick Holly-bush consisting of several trees close together—the stems scored with initials and marks, which is said to have served as a 'post-office' for the passage of letters between the rebels and their friends in the troubled times of 1715 and 1745.

"A curious custom, called 'Holly bussing,' was kept at Netherwitten on Easter Tuesday a few years ago, and may be now for all I know. The young people, headed by the parish clerk playing the fiddle, betook themselves to a wood, where they gathered Holly, with which they afterwards decorated a stone cross in the village, finishing the evening with dancing."

Several remarkable stories setting forth the virtues of the Holly are recorded by Pliny, and may be read in *Holland's Translation of Pliny's Historie of the World*, published in 1601. Of the nature of these stories the succeeding paragraph will give some idea.

I. Aquifolium : Legends, etc.

"In touching the Holy or Hulver Tree if it be planted about an house, whether it be within a city or standing in the country, it serveth for a countercharm and keepeth away all ill spells or inchantments and defends the house from lightning. Pythagorus affirmeth that the flower of this tree will cause water to stand all upon an ice, also that if a staff made thereof, if a man do fling it at any beast what-so-ever, although it chanceth to light short for default of strength in his arms who flung it, will not-with-standing etch forward and roll from the place where it fell upon the earth and approach near to the beast afore-said ; of so admirable a nature is the Holy Tree."

Parkinson in his *Theatrum Botanicum*, 1640, *pp.* 1486-7, after quoting several of these legends, comments on them in the following manner :—
" Superstitions of the Gentiles learned from Pliny,—this I relate that you may understand the fond and vain virtues of those times which I would to God we were not even in these days tainted withall."

In the days when witch-craft was credited, Holly is stated to have been used by witches in their spells and incantations. In *Plant Lore* we learn that " Holly, Juniper and Mistletoe berries were used to form a witch's chain, each link being finished with an acorn." In some of the old Herbals the authors refer to branches of Holly being used as a defence against witch-

53

Holly, Yew and Box

craft, and in reference to this a correspondent in an early volume of the *Floricultural Cabinet* says, "but this precaution has become unnecessary, since old ladies have lost their charming powers and the spells of the youthful fair are too agreeable to be driven from us by a rod of Holly."

In *Plant Lore* the following is also recorded. "The disciples of Zoroaster, or Fire worshippers, believe that the Holly-tree casts no shadow, and both in Persia and India they employ an infusion of its leaves in connection with their religious observances. They also sprinkle the face of a newly born child with water impregnated with Holly bark."

Proverbs

Proverbs bearing reference to the Holly do not seem to be numerous, but the following one about a confirmed prevaricator is very much to the point and worthy of mention :—

"He lees never but when the Hollen is green."

The Holly as a Badge of Cognisance

In Scotland the Holly has always been held in esteem, and it was selected by the Clan Drummond as its badge. Colonel Drummond

I. Aquifolium: Legends, etc.

of Blair Drummond, Perthshire, informs me that it has been the recognised badge of the Clan for many generations, but he never heard why it was chosen.

Many of the Scottish Clans use native trees and animals for their badges, and probably the selection dates back to the days of chivalry, when the mystic meanings attached to the names may have had something to do with their adoption.

In the *Language of Flowers* the Holly is said to mean Foresight.

IX

I. AQUIFOLIUM

The Holly as a Subject for the Poet

POETS have not neglected the Holly, and the following verses of songs, ballads, carols, etc., have been selected for quotation :—

The first consists of four verses from a song entitled *The Ivy and the Holly Girl*, by *John Keegan*, a clever Irish peasant poet who lived in the early part of the last century, and, like Burns, composed his poetry in the intervals of peasant labour. (*See Irish Songs and Song Writers by C. M. Collins, p.* 276.)

"Come buy my nice fresh Ivy and my Holly sprigs so green,
I have the finest branches that ever yet were seen,
Come buy from me, good Christians, and let me home, I pray,
And I'll wish 'Merry Christmas Time' and a 'Happy New
    Year's Day.'

Ah! won't you buy my Ivy? the loveliest ever seen!
Ah! won't you buy my Holly boughs all you who love the
    green!
Do take a little bunch of each, and on my knees I'll pray,
That God may bless your Christmas, and be your 'New
    Year's Day.'

.   .   .   .   .

56

The Holly as a Subject for the Poet

'Twas a dying maiden sung while the cold hail rattled down,
And fierce winds whistled mournfully o'er Dublin's dreary
   town;
One stiff hand clutched her Ivy-sprigs and Holly-boughs so fair
With the other she kept brushing the hail-drops from her hair.

> .   .   .   .   .

I dreamed of wanderings in the woods amongst the Holly
   green;
I dreamed of my own native cot, and porch with Ivy screen;
I dreamed of lights for ever dimmed of hopes that can't
   return—
And dropped a tear on Christmas fires that never more can
   burn."

The next is from a poem of nine verses by
Wm. Harrison, published in the *Floricultural
Cabinet* for 1841, *p.* 88.

"Oh! lively Holly tree
How cheering thou to me
When winter's howling tempests drive around;
How pleasing still to view
Thy sweet unchanging hue
When every other tree is bare and leafless found.

For through the varying year
No yellow tints appear
To streak thy leaves with symptoms of decay;
When spring's mild zephyrs blow
And summer's fervours glow,
The same sweet aspect still dost thou display.

When bounteous autumn pours
Her rich o'erflowing stores,
And the descending vale is redden'd all
Into the gorgeousness
Which does the farmer bless
And loudly on his grateful feeling call

Holly, Yew and Box

When winter's darken'd day
O'er nature's charms bears sway,
And Flora's beauties fall beneath the blast,
Oh! still is to be seen
Thy everlasting green,
Delightful and still lovely to the last."

Shakespere, in *As you Like it*, says—

"Heigh ho! sing heigh ho! unto the green Holly,
Most friendship is feigning, most loving mere folly:
Then, heigh ho, the Holly,
This life is most jolly."

Act ii. Sc. 7.
(Song—" Blow, Blow, Thou Winter Wind.")

The Poet *Southey* takes the variation of leafage on old Hollies for the theme of the following poem.

" O, Reader, hast thou ever stood to see
The Holly Tree?
The eye that contemplates it well perceives
Its glossy leaves,
Order'd by an Intelligence so wise
As might confound the Atheist's sophistries.

Below, a circling fence its leaves are seen
Wrinkled and keen;
No grazing cattle through their prickly round
Can reach to wound;
But as they grow where nothing is to fear,
Smooth and unarmed the pointless leaves appear.

I love to view these things with curious eyes,
And moralise:
And in this wisdom of the Holly Tree

58

The Holly as a Subject for the Poet

Can emblems see,
Wherewith perchance to make a pleasant rhyme
One which may profit in the after time.

Thus though abroad perchance I might appear
Harsh and austere,
To those who on my leisure would intrude
Reserved and rude,
Gentle at home amid my friends I'd be
Like the high leaves upon the Holly Tree."

In *Evelyn's Silva* the following ode is quoted with reference to the snaring of birds with birdlime prepared from Holly bark.

"Alas! In vain with warmth and food
You cheer the Songster of the wood,
The barbarous boy from you prepares
On treacherous twigs his viscous snares.
Yes! the poor bird you nurs'd shall find
Destruction in your rifled rind."

The superstitious legends attached to the Holly are generally beneficial to mankind, and the author of the following lines probably had this in mind when he warned people against mentioning it in a disrespectful manner.

"Her commys Holly, that is so gent
To please all men is his intent,
        Alleluia!
But lord and lady of this hall
Who-so-ever ageynst Holly call,
        Alleluia!
Who-so-ever ageynst Holly do crye
In a lepe shall be hung full hie,
        Alleluia!

Holly, Yew and Box

Who-so-ever ageynst Holly do sing
He may wepe and handys wryng,
Alleluia ! "
See *English Mediæval Ballad in Plant Lore.*

The next verse is attributed to *R. J. Thorn.*

"From every hedge is pluck'd by eager hands
The Holly branch with prickly leaves replete,
And fraught with berries of a crimson hue ;
Which, torn asunder from its parent trunk,
Is straightway taken to the neighb'ring town,
Where windows, mantels, candlesticks, and shelves,
Quarts, pints, decanters, pipkins, basins, jugs,
And other articles of household ware,
The verdant garb confess."

In *Tennyson's In Memoriam* the following lines
occur in stanza *xxx.,*

" With trembling fingers did we weave
The Holly round the Christmas Hearth."

Then in stanza *lxxviii.* we find,

" Again at Christmas did we weave
The Holly round the Christmas Hearth."

Whilst later on in stanza, *cv.,* the lines occur,

" To-night ungather'd let us leave
This Laurel, let this Holly stand."

With writers of Christmas Carols the Holly
has always been a favourite subject, and on many
occasions it has been mentioned, since the first
one we have any record of appeared in the reign
of Henry VI. The last I have noticed is by

60

The Holly as a Subject for the Poet

Lady Montagu of *Beaulieu*, which appeared in the *Daily Mail* on *Christmas* morning 1906. The first two verses of this are as follows :—

> "To many a one were the tidings foretold
> (Oh ! the bright red berry and the green Holly tree !)
> O ! a wonderous appearing to shepherds of old
> (So sing men and maidens, and hearken to me).
>
> To the shepherds affrighted the Angels did say
> (Oh ! the bright red berry and the green Holly tree !)
> To you we bring tidings of great joy this day
> (Then sing men and maidens and hearken to me)."

X

I. AQUIFOLIUM VARIETIES

THE great number of varieties attributed to I. Aquifolium has previously been noted, and some of them are very remarkable, differing so widely from the type that they might well be taken for distinct species were it not for intermediate forms. Whilst admitting the great variability of I. Aquifolium, however, there appears to have been too much lumping done with the garden varieties ; for, whilst the majority of them can be traced to that species fairly accurately, there is a distinct set with large leaves, of which *platyphylla* and *Shepherdi* are examples, which certainly ought not to be classified as varieties of the "Common Holly." In every particular—leaves, growth and fruit—they resemble the Canary Island species, I. platyphylla, more closely than they do I. Aquifolium, and they are evidently varieties of it, or hybrids between that species and the "Common Holly." The connecting link between the two species appears to be the "Balearic Holly," known in gardens as I. A. var. balearica.

WEEPING HOLLY. IN THE ROYAL GARDENS, KEW

I. Aquifolium Varieties

In general appearance it resembles some of the large-leaved forms such as maderensis, whilst herbarium specimens closely approach those of the Canary Island species. In the Kew Herbarium there are many type specimens of I. Aquifolium collected in various parts of Europe, which show great variation in size and spininess of leaf, yet all can be traced to typical I. Aquifolium, except the Balearic forms, which all agree more closely with specimens of other species.

Another point in favour of the large-leaved set being varieties of a species other than I. Aquifolium, or hybrids, is, that all the descendents of I. Aquifolium appear to revert to the type, directly or indirectly, at some period of their existence, whereas the large-leaved Hollies never seem to produce typical "Common Holly" l aves.

There is also a difference in the colour of the ovules, but whether this can be accepted as a good character or not is doubtful; at any rate in all the varieties I have examined, the ovules of the large-leaved set, when well advanced, say the middle of July, are reddish purple in colour, whilst, with two exceptions, all the varieties of the "Common Holly" I have examined have white ovules; the two exceptions are the "yellow fruited variety" and the one called "camelliæfolium," and in these cases the ovules

63

Holly, Yew and Box

are pink. In typical I. Aquifolium, they are invariably white.

A great many of our garden Hollies have been in cultivation for very many years, and their origin is shrouded in mystery. As long ago as 1737 we find that *Miller* in his *Gardener's Dictionary* recognised thirty-three varieties, whilst in 1770 *Hanbury* in his *Complete Book of Gardening, Vol. I. pp.* 217-218 mentions forty-two sorts. Other books published about the latter date enumerate a similar number, though the names do not in all instances correspond, which suggests that the above-mentioned number did not represent the total of known varieties. The greater proportion appear to have been variegated forms, for, of *Hanbury's* forty-two, eight only were green-leaved.

Whilst it is quite probable that the majority of these varieties are still in existence, we cannot vouch for the fact, as very few of the names mentioned in old books are in vogue now. The following is a selection of varieties in cultivation upwards of a century ago.

Painted Lady, Bradley's Best, Wrench's Phyllis, Milkmaid, Box-leaved Green, Chohole, Chimney Sweeper, Glory of the East, Glory of the West, Wife's Holly, Yellow Blotched Hedgehog, Silver Hedgehog, Common Hedgehog, Yellow Berried, Blotched Yellow Berried, White Berried, Mason's Copper Coloured, Sir

I. Aquifolium Varieties

Thomas Frankland's Britain, Bradley's Long Leaved, Bradley's Yellow, Capel's Mottled, Bench's Ninepenny Holly, and Bagshot Holly.

Among these old names there are several that are still applied to varieties, but none of them, or descriptions of any, fit any one of the large-leaved Hollies of the present day, and the majority of them seem to have put in an appearance within the last fifty years. A variety that seems to have been lost, or to have become very uncommon, is that known as "White Berried," whilst the "Yellow Berried" is common.

Collections of Hollies have been formed for upwards of two centuries, but the most complete ones have been those of commercial establishments, and the owners do not seem to have troubled to leave any record to show how various varieties were obtained. One of the earliest collections we find information about is that of a Mr Wrench, who was in business as a nurseryman in Fulham during the latter part of the reign of King Charles II., say 1670 to 1685. He is reported to have been an assiduous collector of varieties, and to have possessed a very fine collection. The planting of the old Elm-trees in St James' Park, London, is stated to have been his work.

Another early collection was that formed by Mr George London at Fulham, about the end of the seventeenth century. This gentleman, in

Holly, Yew and Box

conjunction with Mr Wise, wrote a book called *The Retired Gardener*, in 1706, in which he says, "We have great variety of Hollies in England, and have brought them to more perfection than they are in any other part of the world."

About the middle of the last century Messrs Loddiges are said to have grown seventy or eighty varieties, whilst the names of Fisher and Sibray, Lawson, Waterer, Paul and Cunningham have all been renowned for Hollies in more modern times. One of the most comprehensive commercial collections in the country at the present time is to be found in the Handsworth Nursery of Messrs Fisher, Son and Sibray, Sheffield, a great many original plants of varieties introduced by the firm being on view.

The National collection at Kew is a very fine one, containing nearly all the best marked species, varieties and hybrids.

The fact of so many varieties having originated so long ago makes it impossible to speak with authority about their origin, though it is not difficult to form a fairly circumstantial chain of evidence to account for some of them.

Distinct varieties that have originated directly from I. Aquifolium, either as sports or chance seedlings, are, apparently, comparatively few in number, sub-varieties being much more numerous. Of the direct breaks from the type

66

I. Aquifolium Varieties

the following appear to be the most likely. I. A. ferox, fructu-luteo, pendula, serratifolia, aurea marginata, argentea marginata, donningtonensis, whittinghamensis, argenteo medio-picta, aureo medio-picta, and probably one or two other entire leaved and variegated ones.

The distinct variety known as elliptica, which is much nearer I. dipyrena in all particulars than I. Aquifolium, should be placed under that species as it fits I. dipyrena in the opaque colouring of the leaves, the spines, wood, shape of fruit and time of flowering.

One of the most difficult Hollies to account for is that known as I. A. crassifolia, and it is probable that it may be a species of which the history is lost, for it differs materially from all forms of I. Aquifolium, growth, leafage and fruit, being very distinct and uniform in character, little or no variation occurring. No particulars of its origin can be found, and the first notice of it that I have been able to procure is in *Hanbury's Complete Book of Gardening*, 1770, where it is called the " Saw-leaved Holly " and described as follows. " Saw-leaved Holly is a kind very different from any of the other sorts. The leaves are as long as any of the sorts, very narrow, and of a thick substance. Their edges are formed into the likeness of a saw, though they are not very sharp and prickly. This is a very scarce and valuable Holly, and is by all admired."

E 67

Holly, Yew and Box

Of all the well marked varieties, ferox is probably the oldest, and has been the originator of some of the most distinct and interesting of the garden forms. Its origin is doubtful, though it was probably found wild in France. *Miller*, Martyn's edition, says that Mr George London introduced it from France into English gardens, and he considered it a good species as he found that it came true from seeds. He also reports it as being found in Canada, and as being hardy there. From these two assertions I am inclined to think that Martyn must have confused this with something else, for so far as personal observations go, and from what I can learn from other people, the true " Hedgehog Holly," I. A. ferox, produces male flowers only, and it is not mentioned in lists of N. American trees. As a set off against *Miller's* statement, *Parkinson in 1640* (*Theatrum Botanicum, pp. 1486-7*) gives the variety echinatum, which is synonymous with ferox, and describes it as "a Holly with leaves wholly prickly," and goes on to say, "this differeth not from the ordinary sort, either in body, fruite, roote, or use, only in the leafe, which is no less armed, with sharp prickles all upon as about the edges thereof." From this it was evidently in cultivation before London's time. Parkinson, however, refers to fruit so that it would appear as if a fruiting form was known. There is just the possibility that the two varieties,

I. Aquifolium Varieties

ferox and crassifolia, have been confused, though there is no resemblance between them.

Another very old variety is I. A. fructu-luteo, for in *Cole's History of Plants, published in 1657*, he says, "there may be said to be three sorts of Holly: (1) the Holly-tree without prickles; (2) the Holly with prickly leaves; and (3) the Holly with yellow berries." The latter he states was found growing wild in Wiltshire on the estate of Lord Arundel near Wardour Castle. From this it would appear that Parkinson's echinatum was unknown to Cole.

The numerous varieties can be formed into several distinct groups, which may be recognised by means of size, shape, colour or spininess of leaves, whilst colour of stem also enters into the distinctive marks of some forms. Several of the most distinct varieties of all owe their origin to I. A. ferox, for although widely removed from that variety, connecting links can be found which point plainly to a succession of sports. Thus on one hand we have crispa, a sport from ferox with curly leaves and few spines; scotica, a sport from crispa, with moderately flat leaves which have usually entire margins but with evidences of dentation noticeable here and there; ovata, a most distinct variety, but which gives ample evidence of having been a sport from scotica; whilst from ovata typical "Common Holly" leaves are sometimes borne, though it rarely, if

69

Holly, Yew and Box

ever, happens that "Common Holly" leaves are borne by either of the intermediate varieties.

In this theory of the origin of certain varieties there is one flaw, for, whilst ferox, crispa and ovata are all classed among the varieties which bear staminate flowers, scotica bears female blooms.

Looking in another direction we find that, commencing from ferox, we get crispa with few spines and varieties originating from it with spines developed in a very marked degree but few in number, such as latispina and monstrosa, but which show a tendency to get back to typical I. Aquifolium. The inference is that some untoward condition has caused the abnormal formation of spines in I. A. ferox, and so fixed it that it cannot revert to I. Aquifolium without going through a series of intermediate stages.

Some varieties are so well fixed that variations rarely occur, whilst others vary considerably, whole branches often reverting to typical "Common Holly" or some other variety. The variegated-leaved sorts give ample proof of these peculiarities, for, whilst those forms which have the variegation on the outer parts of the leaves and the inner part green rarely deviate from the typical colour, those varieties which have the centre of the leaf variegated and the border green produce typical green leaves freely.

As the question frequently arises as to which

I. Aquifolium Varieties

are the best fruiting varieties, the following list of male and female sorts has been prepared; it must however be borne in mind that a judicious number of male varieties must be included in collections if the best fruiting results are desired, though it sometimes happens that fruits swell up and mature without containing fertile seeds.

Varieties with male flowers :—

argentea marginata elegantissima.
argentea regina.
aurea angustifolia
aurea medio-picta, in part.
aurea regina.
ciliata.
crispa.
donningtonensis.
ferox.
Fisheri.
Foxii.
grandis.
integrifolia, in part.
laurifolia.
Mundyi.
ovata.
recurva.
Smithiana.

Varieties with female flowers :—

angustifolia.
argentea marginata.
argentea marginata pendula.
argentea medio-picta.
aurea marginata.
aurea marginata bromeliæfolia.
aurea marginata fructu-luteo.
aurea medio-picta, in part.
camelliæfolia.
ciliata major.
crassifolia.
flavescens.
fructu-luteo.
Handsworth New Silver.
integrifolia, in part.

Holly, Yew and Box

Varieties with male flowers :—	Varieties with female flowers :—
Watereriana.	Marnocki.
whittingtonensis.	pendula.
	pendula tricolor.
	scotica.

XI*

I. AQUIFOLIUM VARIETIES—*Continued*

Varieties with Average-Sized Green Leaves

I. **A. alcicornis.** — A distinct large-leaved Holly, remarkable for its very spiny leaves. It is a free growing variety, and one of those in which the young bark is green. The leaves are bright green, 3½ inches long by 1¾ inches broad, oblong obovate in outline, with an entire wedge-shaped base, the rest of the margin furnished with numerous long, narrow, stiff, sharply-pointed spines ⅝ of an inch in length.

I. A. chinensis.—This is a form found in Central China, and resembles the type in many respects. Herbarium specimens, however, suggest a more slender habit and thinner leaves than is usually the case in the species. Small plants in the Coombe Wood nursery also give evidence of these peculiarities.

I. A. costata = "Grecian Holly."—This is one of the varieties sent out from the Handsworth Nurseries, Sheffield. It belongs to the series with purple or reddish-purple bark, while the deep green leaves, which are 2½ inches long and

* Many of the descriptions contained in this chapter are based on those of Thomas Moore's, which appeared in the *Gardeners' Chronicle*, 1874.

Holly, Yew and Box

1¼ inches broad, are oblong acute, furnished with slightly divaricate spines at somewhat distant intervals. It is a freegrowing sort, and has the costa distinctly indicated by a purple line on the back of the leaf.

I. A. fructu-albo = "White-berried Holly."— This plant appears to have been well known a century ago, but is not met with at the present time. It resembled the "Common Holly" in every respect, except that the fruits were white or cream-coloured.

I. A. fructu - aurantiaco = "Orange - berried Holly."—A form of the "Yellow-berried Holly," with deep orange coloured fruits which are sometimes flushed with scarlet. It is evidently a seedling form of the "Yellow-berried Holly."

I. A. fructu-luteo = "Yellow-berried Holly." —This is one of the oldest known varieties of the "Common Holly," and history tells us that it was discovered several centuries ago growing in a wood near Wardour Castle in Wiltshire ; it has also been found wild at Wiston near Buers in Suffolk. The leaves are from 2½ to 3 inches long, ovate in form, and bright green in colour. The margins are generally armed with a moderate number of spines which are slightly divaricate. In general appearance it closely resembles the "Common Holly," its principal difference being in the yellow instead of red fruits.

I. A. Lichtenthalii.—A distinct variety be-

1. A. AQUIFOLIUM, 2. I. A. ALCICORNIS, 3. I. A. ANGUSTIFOLIA A,
4. I. A. ANGUSTIFOLIA B
Reproduced by permission of the Editor of " The Gardeners' Chronicle"

I. Aquifolium Varieties

longing to the large-leaved set of I. Aquifolium. The leaves are oblong, 4 inches long, 1½ inches wide, bright green, regularly armed with moderately strong divaricate spines. The chief peculiarities of the variety are the relative narrowness of the leaves compared with their length, the distinct pale colour of the principal vein, spines, margins and under surface, and the formation of two tiny spines, one on each side near the base of the leaf.

I. A. pendula = " Common Weeping Holly." —The peculiarity of this form is that its branches are pendent; its leaves are deep green, divaricately spiny, and ordinarily from 2 inches to 3 inches long. The bark is deep purple in some cases, purplish in others, and green in others ; while the spines are somewhat broader, and in some cases fewer in number than in the type, though sufficiently numerous to bring it among the many-spined varieties. When well grown it forms a handsome specimen many yards in circumference with an evenly balanced head. As no leading shoot is formed it is necessary to keep a shoot tied up to get height into the plant. In the Gardener's Chronicle for March 6, 1847, p. 158, a record is given by Mr John Booker, gardener to Charles Clarke, Esq., Matlock Bath, of a weeping Holly being found wild in a wood on that estate growing in such a position that it must have grown from a self-sown seed. This

Holly, Yew and Box

is the first record we have been able to obtain of a weeping variety.

I. A. var. Robinsoniana.—This is a very distinct green-leaved form with very ferocious spines. The leaves are deep green and glossy, 3 inches long, and barely 1 inch in width. The margins are undulated, and divided up into numerous divaricate spines often $\frac{1}{2}$ an inch in length, sometimes standing out straight from the margins, at others bent downwards at right angles with the leaf, and at other times turned upwards at the same angle. It is one of the lesser known varieties, and is worth including in select lists.

Varieties with Small, Evenly Spined Green Leaves

I. A. angustifolia = myrtifolia stricta. — An elegant growing variety of narrow pyramidal habit, the bark green or purplish, the leaves lanceolate, or lanceolate ovate, about 1$\frac{1}{2}$ inches long and $\frac{1}{2}$ an inch broad, shining green, with a longish, entire point, and narrow weakish regular marginal spines, from about five to seven on each side of the leaf, and lying in the same plane. It comes near myrtifolia, but has narrower spines, and the elongated entire apex, as shown in the figure marked A, is in general well defined.

I. A. ciliata. = ciliata minor and pyramidalis. —A pretty variety of pyramidal habit and neat growth. The bark is purplish ; the leaves ovate

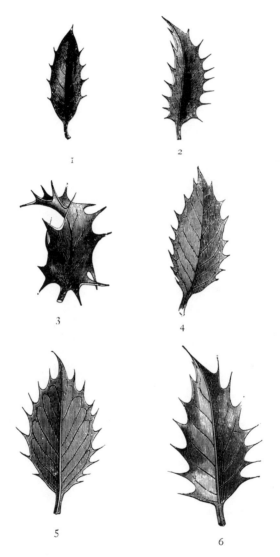

1. I. A. MICROPHYLLA, 2. I. A. SERRATIFOLIA, 3. I. A. RECURVA,
4. I. A. MYRTIFOLIA, 5. I. A. CILIATA, 6. I. A. HANDSWORTHENSIS
Reproduced by permission of the Editor of " The Gardeners' Chronicle"

I. Aquifolium Varieties

or lanceolate, of a shining green, $1\frac{1}{2}$ inches—rarely 2 inches—long, and from $\frac{1}{2}$ to $\frac{3}{4}$ of an inch broad, margined with long, weak, regularly placed spines, which form a kind of fringe to the edge.

I. A. compacta.—A small-leaved sort, with the bark dark purple; the leaves shortly ovate, from a broad base, about $1\frac{1}{4}$ inches long by $\frac{3}{4}$ inch broad, spiny throughout, with the spines comparatively bold, and with a strongly divaricate undulation. It is a distinct-looking form.

I. A. handsworthensis.—This is a green barked variety, which originated in the Handsworth Nurseries of Messrs Fisher & Co. The leaves are ovate-lanceolate, acuminate, of a glossy green, $1\frac{3}{4}$ inches in length, and about $\frac{3}{4}$ inch in breadth, with numerous thickly-set marginal spines, which are projected forwards towards the apex of the leaf, and are moderately divaricate.

I. A. lineata.—This is the smallest-leaved form of the " Common Holly" which we have met with. It is a mere curiosity, and is apt to run out into vigorous branches, so that no doubt it originated as so many varieties have done in a sporting branch. The bark is green; the leaves narrow lanceolate, $\frac{3}{4}$ inch long, flat, evenly edged with minute spines.

I. A. microphylla = angustifolia minor.—A small-leaved sort, forming a compact diminutive bush. The bark is purple; the leaves lanceolate, flat, of a shining green, furnished along the

77

margin with small, distinct spines. The leaves barely exceed an inch in length. Though very distinct, it could only be regarded as a curiosity in a collection of Hollies, being too small to be effective.

I. A. myrtifolia—A small-leaved, neat-growing form, occurring both with green and purplish bark. The leaves are usually from about 1¼ inches to 1½ inches in length, and from ½ inch to ⅝ inch in breadth, ovate-lanceolate, with the margin either entire or with one or two erratic spines, or more commonly in the largest leaves moderately spiny throughout, the spines being usually sub-divaricate, but sometimes nearly flat, especially in the few-spined examples. They are of a bright green colour. This variety appears to come nearest to angustifolia.

I. A. recurva = serratifolia compacta. — This variety which has usually purplish bark, though sometimes green, is harsh-leaved and strongly spined, like serratifolia, but the spines are more divaricate, or appear to be more so, in consequence of the much stronger convex curvature of the leaf in the direction of the midrib, combined with which there is a kind of lateral twist, and also a twisted disposition of the leaves on the stalk. They are ovate-acuminate, of a dull dark green, about 1¼ inches long and ½ an inch broad, spiny throughout the margin, the apex usually terminating in an elongated spine. The con-

I. A. CAMELLIÆFOLIA

I. Aquifolium Varieties

vexity of the leaf surface gives it a kind of channelled appearance from the lifting up of the edges. The plant has a tendency to a dwarfish, dense habit of growth.

I. A. serratifolia.—One of the smaller neat-leaved Hollies, a good deal resembling myrtifolia but differing in its stiffer leaves having a more elongated apex, its more decidedly divaricate spines, and in its tendency to become recurved at the point. This plant is of pyramidal habit and well adapted for training into formal specimens. The bark is green or purplish. The leaves are lance-shaped in outline, about, or rather less, than $1\frac{1}{2}$ inches long, and about $\frac{1}{2}$ inch broad, of a dark glossy green, stiff, the midrib convexly curved so that the leaf-edges are brought up and form a sort of channel of the upper surface, with the numerous regular and rather stout spines moderately divaricate. The same variety is sometimes seen under the name of angustifolia.

Green-Leaved Varieties Recognised by the Majority of their Leaves being Spineless or Bearing but a few Spines only

I. A. camelliæfolium = magnifica, laurifolium longifolium, heterophylla major.—Without doubt this is one of the most ornamental of all the varieties of the " Common Holly." It is of vigorous habit and grows naturally into a hand-

Holly, Yew and Box

some, shapely pyramid, retaining at all seasons a dense leafage. The bark of the young wood is purple. The leaves are oblong or elliptic, acuminate, of a dark, olive green and very glossy. They are from 3½ to 5 inches long, and 1½ to 2 inches across, the margins either smooth and spineless throughout, or with an erratic spine or two, or with the lower part entire and the upper with some 4 or 5 well developed undulating spines on each side, or rarely armed on both margins throughout the entire length. It is a female variety and bears larger and darker coloured fruits than the type.

I. A. crispa = marginata, contorta, tortuosa, calamistrata, and " Screw-leaved Holly."—A fine, well marked Holly, with the bark of the young shoots purple and the leaves blunt-ended and spirally twisted, having, moreover, a certain degree of rugosity or asperity on the upper surface, as if it were trying to throw up the superficial spines characteristic of the " Hedge-hog Holly." The leaves are even more variable than in other varieties and from one tree many different types of leaf may be gathered ; some approach closely to ferox, others to scotica, others to latispina, and so on. In some cases the margin is entire, in others rudimentary spines are produced, whilst again, one or two erratic spines may be abnormally developed. The chief peculiarities of the variety are the deep, glossy green colour, the

I. I. A. CRISPA A, 2. I. A. CRISPA B, 3. I. A. CRISPA C,
4. I. A. DONNINGTONENSIS A.
Reproduced by permission of the Editor of " The Gardeners' Chronicle"

I. Aquifolium Varieties

thickened margins, spiral twisting of the leaf blade and the surface spines borne by some of the leaves.

I. A. donningtonensis. — This is another of the Handsworth batch, having been sent out by Messrs Fisher & Co. The plant is of free, pyramidal growth, and is a very distinct and effective variety in collections. The bark is of a very dark purple colour; and the leaves, which are variable in size and form, and stout in texture, are also of a dull purplish green, so that the bush contrasts strongly with the bright green varieties. The general outline of the leaves is lanceolate, but they are not unfrequently turned to one side so as to become sickle-like, and they have also frequently a small lateral and often falcate lobe at the base ; they average about 2 inches in length and ¾ inch in breadth, but sometimes slightly exceed these dimensions ; the margin is frequently quite entire or with a few (1-5) erratic spines, but occasionally the spines become more numerous, and sometimes the margin is furnished throughout with them, the spines when present being strong and much divaricate.

The spiny leaves bear much resemblance in form to those of whittingtonensis, but their thicker texture and purple hue at once distinguishes them, while in the plant the presence and prevalence of the entire or slightly spiny leaves furnish additional evidence as to the name.

Holly, Yew and Box

In this variety the midrib shows a streak of purple along the back of the leaf.

From the Lawson Nursery Company Mr Moore received specimens, under the name of I. A. whittingtonensis monstrosa, a form of donningtonensis which differed only in the fasciated growth of the branches, but whether or not this was confined to the leading shoots, or occurred throughout the plant, we are not informed.

I. A. Fisheri.—This also is one of the many fine varieties raised and sent out from the Handsworth Nurseries. Our authentic samples have green bark; and the leaves, which are variable in character, are about 2½ inches long and 1¼ inches wide, of a very dark green colour and coriaceous texture, ovate, with a somewhat acuminate apex, occasionally entire, with a thickened margin, somewhat spiny throughout, with strong, much divaricated spines, more commonly with 1-2 to 5-6 spines along the margins, and an entire acuminate point. It is a bold, free growing, and a handsome sort. Although the bark is usually green, specimens have been noted with purplish bark.

I. A. heterophylla = heterophylla major.— This variety has considerable resemblance to laurifolia; but the leaves are shorter and comparatively broader. The bark is usually purple; and the leaves, which are ovate or elliptic ovate, average 2½ inches in length, by 1 or 1½ inches in

3

1. I. A. WHITTINGTONENSIS, 2. I. A. DONNINGTONENSIS B.
3. I. A. HETEROPHYLLA
Reproduced by permission of the Editor of " The Gardeners' Chronicle "

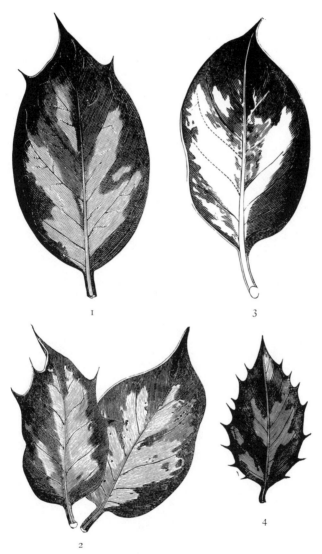

1 & 2. I. A. HETEROPHYLLA AUREO-PICTA, 3. I. A. LAURIFOLIA
AUREO-PICTA, 4. I. A. MYRTIFOLIA AUREO-MACULATA A.
Reproduced by permission of the Editor of " The Gardeners' Chronicle"

I. Aquifolium Varieties

width, sometimes measuring 2¾ inches by 1½ inches; they are dark green, somewhat twisted near the point, and either entire or (intermixed on the same twigs) distinctly spinose, very rarely— but occasionally—spiny throughout; the spines, when present, are strongly developed and divaricate, generally distant, and always irregularly disposed. It is a free-growing and effective Holly.

I. A. integrifolia = senescens, rotundifolia.— In this variety the bark is purple, and the leaves ovate, entire, thick in texture, with a somewhat thickened margin, dark green, 2 inches long and 1 inch broad, having a slight twist, the point being sometimes acute, as in the annexed figure, sometimes bluntly rounded. It has something of the character of scotica, but the leaves are not so decidedly rounded or twisted, and they are also somewhat larger. The Lawson Company's rotundifolia, as contributed to Mr Moore, does not appear to present any tangible difference from the variety known as integrifolia.

I. A. laurifolia = "Smooth-leaved Holly."—A well-marked and well-known variety, one of the commonest and best of the entire-leaved type, but, like most others, varying a good deal in the actual armature of selected leaves. The plant is of erect, tall growth, but rather open and irregular, a fault which, however, can be remedied by the use of the knife. The bark is dark purple. The leaves also are of a dark green hue, and very glossy; they vary from about 2 inches to 3 inches in length, and in form from ovate to oblong-lanceolate or elliptic, and they are usually quite entire, rarely with from one to six marginal spines, and occasionally but very rarely spiny throughout, the surface being either flat or slightly undulated.

I. A. laurifolia fructu-luteo. — This variety differs from the preceding mainly in the colour of its berries, which are yellow, instead of red, and in the green bark of its young shoots.

I. A. Marnocki.—A large leaved form of the "Common Holly" with the majority of the leaves spineless. The foliage is almost as large as that of camelliæfolium but less dense and ornamental. The leaves are from 4 to 4½ inches long and 2 inches wide, oval and acute with a peculiar twist about the middle. The margins are usually thick and spineless, occasionally however a few erratically placed spines are borne and more rarely the margins are well and regularly armed with strong, divaricate spines. The bark is green on the under side of the branch and purplish on the upper side.

I. A. scotica = Dahoon, *Hort.*—A very distinct and well-marked Holly, and very effective in plantations, being of free erect growth, and densely clothed with very dark green, glossy leaves. The bark of the young growth is of a dark purple colour. The leaves are oblong-

I & 2. TYPES OF LEAVES FOUND ON I. A. FISHERI

Reproduced by permission of the Editor of " The Gardeners' Chronicle "

I. Aquifolium Varieties

obovate, bluntish, rounded at the apex, $1\frac{1}{2}$ inch to 2 inches long, and $\frac{3}{4}$ inch to 1 inch broad, leathery, the margins entire, thickened, wavy, the apex usually blunt, but occasionally with a short spine, or with a cup-like thickening, and the margin moreover bears an occasional but very rare erratic spine.

I. A. Smithiana.—A distinct variety, with narrow leaves, forming the green counterpart of donningtonensis. The bark is green or sometimes tinged with reddish purple ; the leaves are lanceolate, from 2 to $2\frac{1}{2}$ inches long, by $\frac{3}{4}$ to an inch in width, of a bright glossy green colour, with distant, irregular, weakish spines, which are moderately divaricate. The leaves are comparatively thin in texture.

I. A. whittingtonensis. — A small - leaved and very elegant Holly, with purple bark, and lanceolate or elliptic-ovate, thinnish leaves, averaging $2\frac{1}{4}$ inches long and $\frac{5}{8}$ inch in width, but sometimes as much as 3 inches long, and about an inch wide ; these are furnished with numerous stiff, divaricate spines, the spines being often unequally disposed. The leaves are of a dark shining green, and are sometimes rather recurved. It is one of the Handsworth varieties, and quite distinct in character, though apparently occasionally mixed up with donningtonensis, which is altogether a much darker-hued plant.

Holly, Yew and Box

Green-Leaved Varieties with Abnormal Development of Spines

I. A. Beetii.—A very peculiar looking variety, raised in the Handsworth nurseries. It is green barked, with very short, dark green, glossy leaves, nearly circular in outline, about 1½ inches long by 1¾ inches wide, strongly spinose at the edge, the spines very much divaricate. The leaves are stout in texture, with thickened margins. This Holly is remarkably distinct in character, its peculiarity being the shortness and bluntness of the leaves.

I. A. ferox = echinata of some gardens.— This variety, in consequence of the prickly surface of its convex leaves, is commonly called the Hedgehog Holly. The bark of the young shoots is purple. The leaves are ovate-oblong or narrowly ovate, 2 inches to 2½ inches long, much acuminate, with strongly developed, divaricate, marginal spines, the surface, which is more or less convex, being echinate or furnished with stiff erect bristles, whence the name of Hedgehog Holly which is applied to it. The acuminately spiny apex and the convex, echinately spiny surface of the leaves of this variety are its chief distinguishing features. It grows to a considerable size.

I. A. hastata = latispina minor, latispina pygmæa, latispina nana, and kewensis.—A very distinct, small-leaved Holly, sent out by Messrs

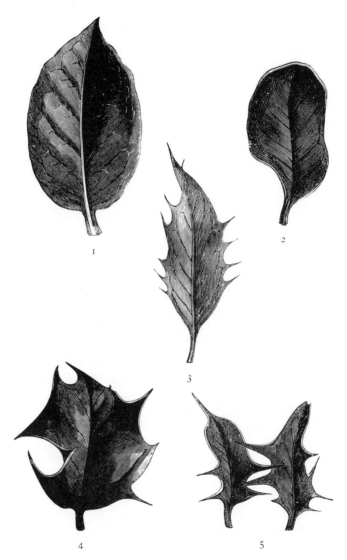

1. I. A. INTEGRIFOLIA, 2. I. A. SCOTICA, 3. I. A. SMITHIANA,
4. I. A. BEETII, 5. I. A. HASTATA

Reproduced by permission of the Editor of " The Gardeners' Chronicle"

I. Aquifolium Varieties

Fisher, Holmes & Co., and remarkable for its purple bark, and the dark green tint of its small peculiarly shaped foliage. The leaves vary from ¾ inch to 1¼ inches in length, and are about ½ inch in breadth irrespective of the spines, which are large and very prominent for the size of the leaf, and consist usually of one or two pairs on each side at the base, but occasionally more, the upper half of the leaf forming a large, entire, oblong, bluntish lobe, not unfrequently emarginate ; hence the whole leaf in the case of those which are few-spined below, and have the apex entire, has a strongly marked hastate figure. The plant appears to be of rather dwarf habit, but is one of the most distinct in character of all the green-leaved varieties. Mr Moore received this variety from the collection at Ochtertyre under the name of heterophylla, which is a very different thing. This variety is so utterly unlike the broad-leaved latispina in aspect and general character, that we prefer to adopt the highly suggestive name, hastata, which it bears in some collections. M. Lœsener gave the varietal name of kewensis a few years ago.

I. A. latispina.—A grand and most effective Holly, being of free growth with a fine pyramidal habit. The bark of the young shoots is dark purple. The leaves vary from about 2 inches to 2½ inches long, and from 1 inch to 1½ inches broad ; they are somewhat quadrate in their

Holly, Yew and Box

general outline, with a very long, acuminate, spiny point which is generally decurved, and a few (about two or three) marginal spines, which are broad and elongated, commonly deflexed but sometimes erect, occasionally hooked backwards with a rounded shoulder, and altogether so various in form and so misshapen as to have quite a grotesque appearance. The colour is a very deep glossy green, and the texture is leathery, with a thickened margin, while the whole blade of the leaf is in some instances slightly twisted. Sometimes the margin is merely wavy without spines, save the long terminal one, and the quadrate general outline of the leaf is then more strongly marked. Its appearance suggests that it originated as a sport from crispa. A form is known under the name of major; this has larger leaves than the type

I. A. monstrosa. — This is a well-marked variety, evidently allied to latispina, with which it is sometimes confounded, and also to trapeziformis, but differing in the constantly numerous spines, which are usually few in the varieties just mentioned. The bark of the young shoots is green or purple, or sometimes greenish purple; and the leaves, which are about 2½ inches long and 1 inch broad (not measuring the spines), are of an oblong outline, much acuminated, of a dark green colour, with numerous strongly developed spines at the margin, most of them being directed

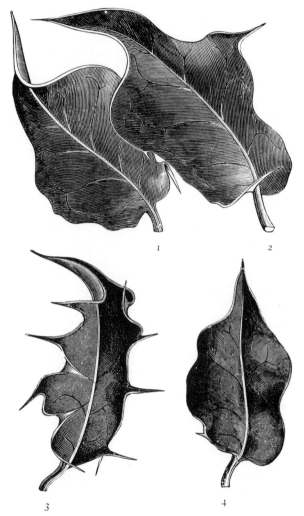

1 & 2. I. A. LATISPINA, 3. I. A. MONSTROSA, 4. I. A. TRAPEZIFORMIS

Reproduced by permission of the Editor of " The Gardeners' Chronicle"

I. Aquifolium Varieties

upwards; the terminal one, however, which tips the long acuminated apex, is pointed downwards. It is a free growing, fine-looking, and very characteristic Holly. We learn from Messrs Fisher, Holmes & Co., that this variety was sent out by them.

I. A. trapeziformis. -- The affinity of this Holly is with montrosa and latispina, coming nearer to the latter, but having smaller leaves with fewer and less grotesquely placed spines. The bark of the young wood is purple. The leaves have a quadrate or squarish limb, bearing a strongly developed terminal spine forming an acuminate point, which is more or less recurved, and generally inclined to one side, the obliquity thus produced having apparently suggested the name; they are about 2 inches in length, by 1 inch in breadth, of a very deep green colour, and have a wavy margin with occasionally one or two erratic divaricate spines.

Other Green-Leaved Varieties

I. A. ciliata major.—A free growing vigorous variety, the young shoots of which have purple bark. The leaves are ovate or ovate-oblong, flattish, margined in a ciliate manner with long, crowded, broad-based, plane spines, the basal portion of the leaf usually entire, and the apex more or less prolonged. The colour is a dark glossy green, with here and there an olive tinge; altogether it is a very distinctly marked and desirable variety.

Holly, Yew and Box

I. A. crassifolia = serrata, "Saw-leaved Holly" and "Leather-leaf Holly."—It is with some reluctance that we keep this as a variety of I. Aquifolium for it is dissimilar to all other varieties in every respect. The growth is looser, individual shoots stouter, the leaves different in outline and texture, exhibiting no real variation, never producing sports and never showing any tendency to produce leaves anything like the "Common Holly," The fruit is also quite different in shape, being peculiarly flattened. It is, however, difficult to associate it with any other species and as it rarely bears fertile seeds it is almost impossible to test it in that way. It has purple bark and lanceolate leaves, the latter being very thick in texture, $1\frac{1}{2}$ to 2 inches long, of a dull green colour, the tips often recurved, and the margins furnished with prominent, dull, saw-like teeth, which have a solid looking appearance quite different from any other variety. It has been known for upwards of a century.

I. A. Foxii.—This variety which is tolerably well marked, has the bark of the young shoots purple. The leaves are ovate, stoutish in texture, 2 to $2\frac{1}{2}$ inches long, with rather distant, regular, plane, fully developed spines, appearing somewhat like ovata, but as if longer spines had been added to its margin. The leaves are of a bright and very glossy green.

I. A. "Oak Vale."—A distinct Holly, probably

90

I. I. A. FOXII, 2. I. A. OVATA A, 3. I. A. OVATA B,
4. I. A. CILIATA MAJOR
Reproduced by permission of the Editor of "The Gardeners' Chronicle"

I. Aquifolium Varieties

a chance hybrid, which originated in Messrs G. Cunningham & Son's nursery. It is of vigorous habit and is conspicuous by reason of its deep green colour and uniformly shaped leaves. These are from 3 to 3½ inches long and 1¾ to 2 inches wide, evenly armed with moderate sized spines most of which lie in the same plane. The apex is acute.

I. A. oblata.—Under this name we have received a distinct form from Messrs Little & Ballantyne. In shape the leaves are very like those of ovata but are only from 1¼ to 1¾ inches long and ¾ inch wide. They are broadly ovate, with short, evenly disposed spines and are of a bright green colour, so differing from ovata which is dark green.

I. A. ovata.—A remarkably distinct Holly, having the bark of the young shoots purple, and the leaves of a deep opaque green. The leaves are of moderate and fairly even size about 2½ inches long, ovate, very thick in texture, with regular, angular, scarcely spiny teeth, the sinuses between the teeth being even more regular and pronounced than in the illustration. It is a slow growing variety, but so distinct that it should never be omitted in making a selection of dissimilar forms. Usually little variation is detected in the leaves, but occasionally, on old specimens, branches bearing typical "Common Holly" leaves are to be found.

91

XII*

I. AQUIFOLIUM VARIETIES—*Continued*

Silver Variegated Varieties with the Marking in the Centres of the Leaves

I. A. argentea medio - picta = medio-picta, albo - picta, " Milkmaid " and " Silver Milkmaid."—A well - known and handsomely variegated Holly, the fault of which is that the variegation is rather apt to run out, unless the tendency thereto is timely checked. It has green bark and ovate or cuneately-ovate leaves 1½ to 2 inches long, and about an inch broad, with very strong and much divaricated spines. The colour is dark green at the edge, with a large central blotch of creamy white which is irregular in shape, size and position, but is frequently confined to the basal half of the leaf.

I. A. Ingramii.—A very distinct, small-leaved Holly, with purple bark. The leaves are elliptic ovate, 1¼ inches long, about ½ an inch wide, evenly bordered with spines ; the disk is of a dark olive-green, somewhat mottled and rugose, the teeth and margins greyish white, the markings being freckly with no distinct outline.

* Many of the descriptions contained in this chapter are based on those of Thomas Moore's, which appeared in the *Gardeners' Chronicle*, 1875.

I. I. A. CRASSIFOLIA B, 2. I. A. ARGENTEA MEDIO-PICTA, 3. I. A. ANGUSTI-
FOLIA ALBO-MARGINATA, 4. I. A. ARGENTEA LONGIFOLIA, 5. I. A·
ARGENTEA MARGINATA LATIFOLIA
Reproduced by permission of the Editor of " The Gardeners' Chronicle"

I. Aquifolium Varieties

I. A. Wiseana = "Wise's Holly." — A fine ornamental variety distinguished by its green bark, and by the outline of its leaves, which are not narrowed to the base. The leaves are ovate, of a dark green colour, with a large creamy white centre, 2¾ inches long ; the margins spiny and wavy, but the spines are less divaricate than on most of the other varieties, and occasionally, but not frequently, the leaves are few-spined. It is a handsome Holly, of tall pyramidal habit.

Silver Variegated Varieties with the Principal Variegation on the Margins of the Leaves

I. A. albo-lineata.—A variety of the silver-edged race, with green bark to the young shoots, ovate leaves, which are slightly wavy, with narrow slender spines, about 2 inches long, 1½ inches wide, the disk greyish mottled green, with a rather indistinct margin of creamy white.

I. A. angustifolia albo marginata = serratifolia albo marginata.—A pretty little shrub with purple bark, the twigs of which are erect. The leaves are similar in size and shape to those of angustifolia but the disk is mottley green, and the margin creamy white, most strongly developed at the apex.

I. A. argentea longifolia = longifolia argentea. —A striking looking variety of vigorous habit, having the young bark purple or purplish. The leaves are elliptic or elliptic-ovate, fully 3 inches

93

Holly, Yew and Box

long, with few long, irregular and unequal, much divaricated spines, the disk mottled and dashed with greyish green and the margin narrowly belted with creamy white which is irregular in width, and sometimes breaks out into broader patches. A well-marked and ornamental form.

I. A. argentea marginata = argentea lato-marginata, argentea, variegata argentea, and albo-marginata.—This is the commonest of the silver variegated sorts and varies somewhat in appearance. The bark of the young wood is green. The leaves are broadly ovate, 2 to 2½ inches long, with usually somewhat numerous but irregular divaricate spines, sometimes with the spines fewer or almost wanting; the colour dark green, with the disk slightly mottled, and with an irregular narrowish silvery margin. It is a fruiting variety.

I. A. argentea marginata elegantissima.—A very striking variety, in which the bark of the young shoots is green. The leaves are elliptic-oblong, 2 inches long and 1 inch broad, with bold and regularly developed spines, which become divaricate from the wavy surface of the leaf; the disk is dark green, mottled with grey, and with a broadish tolerably even edging of creamy white.

I. A. argentea marginata erecta = "Upright Silver-striped."—In this variety, which was introduced to the Knap Hill Nursery by Mr R.

1 & 2. I. A. ARGENTEA MARGINATA PECTINATA MINOR, 3. I. A. ARGENTEA
MARGINATA PENDULA, 4. I. A. ARGENTEA REGINA, 5. I. A. ARGENTEA
MARGINATA PURPUREA

Reproduced by permission of the Editor of " The Gardeners' Chronicle"

I. Aquifolium Varieties

Godfrey, the leaves are about 2 inches long, flat, with a very regular marginal series of strongly-developed spines, in this respect somewhat resembling "Handsworth New Silver;" the leaves have a mottled green centre, and a broad creamy white margin. It is one of the berry bearing forms.

I. A. argentea marginata latifolia = latifolia argentea.—This comes near Silver Queen but has shorter leaves, with bold striking variegation. The bark of the young shoots is purple. The leaves are broadly-ovate, 2 inches long by 1½ inches broad, with a purple petiole, the disk dark green, very much mottled with green and grey, and with an irregular creamy white margin, here and there broadish, the edge armed with rather narrow wavy spines, variable in position.

I. A. argentea marginata major. — A bold vigorous growing variety with green bark. The leaves are ovate or oblong, 3½ to 4 inches long, with much divaricate, large, triangular spines; the surface is green, with a comparatively narrow and rather irregular silver edge. It is a fruiting variety and has a more pendulous habit than I. A. argentea marginata.

I. A. argentea marginata pectinata minor = pectinata minor, argentea angustifolia and "Narrow-leaved Silver-striped." — A green barked variety of free growth, dense and compact in

Holly, Yew and Box

habit. The leaves are ovate or ovate-lanceolate, 1¼ to 1¾ inches long, less than 1 inch wide ; the spines numerous, rather strongly developed for the size of the leaf, usually flattish, but sometimes partially wavy ; the disk green, mottled, and streaked with grey, and with a broadish, tolerably regular edge of creamy white. One of the most desirable and ornamental of the smaller-leaved silver variegated varieties.

I. A. argentea marginata pendula = " Perry's Weeping," pendula argentea, pendula variegata, alba marginata pendula, Perryana major, pendula elegans marginata, and pendula argentea purpurea.—A fine and well-known variety of weeping habit. It is of vigorous constitution and belongs to the purple-barked series. The leaves are 2½ to 3 inches long, ovate or ovate-oblong, the margins furnished with large conspicuous spines, somewhat less crowded and regular than in the variety " Handsworth New Silver "; the surface is green, freely blotched with greyish-green, and the margin is irregularly but often boldly marked with creamy white.

I. A. argentea marginata purpurea.—A fine broad-leaved variety with purple bark. The leaves are broadly ovate, 2¼ inches long and about 1½ inches broad, the disk mottled with dark green and greyish-green and the edge flat and spiny, irregularly belted with creamy white. Very distinct as regards the form of leaf.

96

I. Aquifolium Varieties

I. A. argentea regina = " Silver Queen " and spinus argentea.—A grand Holly, and taken altogether, the best of the varieties having silver-edged leaves. The bark of the young wood is purplish or reddish brown. The leaves are broadly ovate, 2¾ inches long, and 1¾ inches broad, with strongly developed and tolerably evenly placed spines, which are much divaricate; the disk is of a dark green, with patches of greyish-green, and there is a broad irregular, but well-defined edging of creamy white, which is most strongly developed at the apex. Its bold leaves and well-defined, striking marking fully entitle it to the first place in the series to which it belongs.

I. A. ferox argentea = " Silver-striped Hedgehog Holly."—In this the leaves are of the same size, shape, and spininess of the common ferox, but the majority of the spines are silver coloured and there is a broad and irregular margin of the same colour, the disk being deep green. It is an effective variety.

I. A. grandis = " Black-wooded Silver-striped." —Mr Moore describes two varieties as argentea elegantissima one with green and the other with purple bark. They are quite distinct in general appearance and the dark stemmed one is known now as I. A. grandis. It is a well-marked variety with elliptic or elliptic ovate leaves, 2¼ to 4 inches long, with unequal but divaricating spines, sometimes few, sometimes wanting on one side, generally few and distant, rarely evenly distributed throughout, all directed forward; the colour is dark green on the central part, with grey blotches, and the margin is creamy white, irregularly laid on, frequently most thoroughly developed towards the tip, but more or less regular throughout.

I. A. "Handsworth New Silver."—This remarkably handsome "Silver Holly" was introduced by the Handsworth firm of nurserymen many years ago. It has been confused with the green leaved variety, I. A. handsworthensis, and called I. A. handsworthensis argentea variegata. In Moore's Monograph it is figured as handsworthensis but it is a totally different plant from that variety. It is a purple-barked variety and a free and vigorous grower. The leaves are elliptic-oblong, $2\frac{1}{2}$ to $3\frac{1}{2}$ inches long, margined with very prominent spines, which lie in the plane of the leaf with scarcely any tendency to divarication; the disk is mottled with green and greyish-green, and there is a distinct and tolerably even margin of creamy white, the strong conspicuous marginal spines being also white.

I. A. laurifolia sulphurea = laurifolia argentea. —A variety which has the young bark purple. The leaves are oblong, almost acuminate, sometimes slightly obovate, or ovate, occasionally oblique, entire or with a spine set here and

98

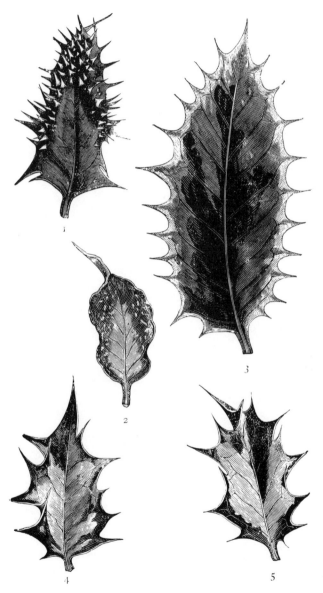

1. I. A. FEROX ARGENTEA, 2. I. A. CRISPA AUREO-PICTA,
3. I. A. HANDSWORTH NEW SILVER, 4 & 5. I. A. AUREA MEDIO-PICTA.
Reproduced by permission of the Editor of "The Gardeners' Chronicle"

I. Aquifolium Varieties

there, but very few in number. The disk is of a mottled green, surrounded at the edge by a broadish unequal band of sulphur-yellow. It is paler than the golden laurifolia, but scarcely enough to be called silver-leaved.

XIII *

I. AQUIFOLIUM VARIETIES—*Continued*

Golden Variegated Varieties with Green Margins

I. A. aurea medio - picta = aurea picta, aurea picta spinosa and "Gold Milkmaid."—This is a distinct and beautiful variety which exhibits some diversity in size and colouring of foliage. It frequently occurs as a sport on I. Aquifolium, and this, with a slight variation in the size of the leaves and spines, has occasioned the adoption of several different names. It is recognised by means of the disk being irregularly marked by a large, deep golden blotch which frequently occupies more than half the surface whilst the irregular margin is of a dark glossy green. There are both male and female forms.

I. A. aurea medio-picta latifolia. — This is the best form of "Gold Milkmaid" and is distinguished from other forms by means of its large, flattened leaves. The spines are variable in number and position, but they are stout, well developed and divaricate, generally wanting at the rounded base of the leaf, and sometimes confined to a few near the apex. The broad

* Many of the descriptions contained in this chapter are based on those of Thomas Moore, which appeared in the *Gardeners' Chronicle*, 1876.

I. Aquifolium Varieties

disk of gold occupies most of the surface whilst there is a narrow irregular margin of green. It is a most effective variety.

I. A. crispa aureo - picta = tortuosa aureo-picta, contorta aurea picta, marginata aureo-picta, crispum aureum, recurva aurea, tortuosa picta, and "Gold-blotched Screw Holly."—In this variety the bark of the young wood is purplish. The leaves are twisted and coriaceous, with a thickened margin, as in I. A. crispa, glossy and puckered on the surface, almost shapeless from the twisting and the irregular development of the spines, which are sometimes wholly wanting the thickened edge being undulated, and sometimes sparingly produced in an altogether erratic manner. The marginal portions are deep green, whilst the disk is marbled with yellow and pale green, the yellow predominating near the base. It is doubtless a sport from I. A. ferox aurea and like that variety is subject to the production of green branches.

I. A. flavescens = aurantiaca, lutescens, "Copper-coloured," "Moonlight Holly," flavum and "Bronze Holly."—In this there is no distinctly defined variegation, but a flush of a yellowish hue is spread over more or less of the leaf surface, the yellow colouring being not only variable in extent but also in position. The bark on the older parts is purplish whilst that of the youngest shoots is often yellowish. The

Holly, Yew and Box

leaves are oblong-ovate, sometimes as much as 3½ inches long, thick in texture, strongly waved, with prominent marginal spines, resembling in form generally, those of the "Common Holly." The surface is unequally flushed with a dull bronzy-yellow hue, which sometimes occupies the upper half of the leaf, sometimes an irregular portion near the centre, other portions of the surface remaining green. This colouring is most strongly marked on the young and year old growths, the older persistent leaves becoming gradually greener. The flush of colours renders this a conspicuous variety and has been likened to "pale moonlight," hence the common name "Moonlight Holly." Shoots bearing leaves of a similar colour may sometimes be found on the purple-barked forms of the aurea marginata group.

I. A. ferox aurea = ferox aurea-picta, ferox foliis aureis, and "Gold-blotched Hedgehog."— This is a well-marked and very handsome Holly, commonly known as the "Gold-blotched Hedge-hog." It has the young bark purple. The leaves are oblong or ovate-oblong, very strongly spined both at the margin and on the upper surface ; they are also strongly waved, and more or less recurved longitudinally. The surface is of a rich deep green, and the green spines which bristle from its surface have pale tips, while on the plain central portion near the base of the leaf-blade is to be found a conspicuous blotch of

1. I. A. AUREA MEDIO-PICTA, 2. I. A. AUREA MEDIO-PICTA LATIFOLIA,
3. I. A. FLAVESCENS, 4. I. A. FEROX AUREA
Reproduced by permission of the Editor of " The Gardeners' Chronicle "

I. Aquifolium Varieties

golden yellow. The convexed bristling surface is well expressed by the term "hedgehog," applied to this, as well as to the green-leaved and silver-margined forms all of which are desirable plants. This particular variety differs considerably in size and form of leaf.

I. A. heterophylla aureo-picta = pictum.—Mr Moore gives the following description of this variety. "This variety, which in its markings is similar to I. A. laurifolia aureo-picta, occurs in the Ochtertyre collection under the name of medio-picta aurea; it differs, however, essentially from laurifolia aureo-picta in having the bark of the young wood green instead of purple. The leaves are ovate, sometimes inclining to elliptic, flat, and toothless, or with one or two marginal teeth; they are 2½ inches long, dark green at the edge, often blotched with paler grey-green in the centre, and there conspicuously marked with a broad, unequally developed, feathery blotch of bright yellow, which makes it a very effective plant. At Ochtertyre, where there is a tree 20 feet high, it is noted as a sterile variety."

I. A. laurifolia aureo-picta = laurifolia aurea variegata.—A handsomely blotched Holly, the young shoots of which have a purplish or reddish brown bark. The leaves are ovate, 2¾ inches long, dark green at the margins, and marked with a bold, irregular, more or less feathered blotch of deep golden-yellow.

103

Holly, Yew and Box

I. A. myrtifolia aureo-maculata.—This is a bright looking variety with the bark of the young wood purple. The leaves are ovate, an inch to an inch and a half long, stout in texture, of a glossy dark green, distinctly marked by broad clearly defined blotches of deep yellow in the centre or disk, the markings very variable in form and arrangement ; the margin is furnished with numerous even spines, which are developed in the plane of the leaf or nearly so. It is one of the handsomer of the small Hollies.

I. A. scotica aureo-picta = scotica aurea and scurtica picta.—A handsome variety that originated in the Cheshunt Nursery of Mr Paul. Its leaves are similar in outline and texture, with the same thick margin as I. A. scotica, but the disks are heavily blotched or striped with gold. Sometimes the gold colour predominates over the green, the latter being merely a narrow, irregular margin, but more often green and gold are fairly evenly represented. The green colouring is usually of two shades, a deep olive on the outer part with yellowish green patches where the gold is joined. It is a neat growing Holly and worthy of extended culture.

I. A. serratifolia aureo maculata = Gold-blotched serratifolia. A minute - leaved, gold-blotched variety with purple bark. The leaves are lanceolate, an inch to an inch and a half long, and barely half an inch broad, with a few

I. Aquifolium Varieties

distant, moderately developed spines lying in the plane of the leaf, the somewhat extended apex being entire. The colour is a dark glossy green, decorated, sometimes in the centre, sometimes near the edge, with bands or fillets of gold, the markings being very dissimilar in different leaves. It is less effective than some of the other small-leaved varieties.

Varieties with Golden Variegated Margins

I. A. **angustimarginata** = angustimarginatum aureum and aurea vestita.—This variety has purplish or reddish purple bark. The leaves are elliptic lanceolate or ovate lanceolate, with numerous, strong, and widely set spines, which are moderately divaricate, the disk dark green mottled with grey, the margin yellow but irregular in width and usually narrow.

I. A. **aurea marginata** = marginata aurea.— In its widest sense this name includes a large proportion of the golden variegated Hollies, but a number of the most distinct forms, have been selected at various times for further descriptive titles. There are still however many Hollies under this name, which show slight variations, but are not distinct enough for other names so some considerable latitude has to be allowed this variety. Typical aurea marginata has usually green bark and large leaves, the latter being 2½ to 3 inches long and 1½ inches wide, with stout,

Holly, Yew and Box

divaricate, unequally distributed spines. The disk is dark green with grey-green mottlings and the golden edge moderately narrow and unequal, but rather strongly developed about the tip. Sometimes the leaves are entirely golden.

I. A. aurea marginata angustifolia = aurea angustifolia, and angustifolia aurea marginata. This is a well-marked Holly, with a purplish-red, or occasionally green bark. The leaves are elliptic-oblong, acuminate, 1½ to 2¼ inches long and scarcely an inch in breadth, with a spiny edge, which is but moderately wavy; the centre is strongly marked with pale green, and the narrow but even margin is of a deep gold colour. This plant must not be confused with angustifolia aurea maculata for it is not a form of the green variety known as angustifolia.

I. A. aurea marginata bromeliæfolia = bromeliæfolia aureo-marginata.—A purple barked variety with flattish, broadly ovate leaves, 2 to 2½ inches long and 1¼ to 1½ inches wide with fairly evenly produced, marginal spines. The disk is slightly mottled with grey green on a dark ground and there is a narrow and irregular golden margin, the colouring being most distinct near the apex. Although not a very ornamental variety it is worth including in collections on account of its distinct appearance and the uniformity of the leaves. Fruits are borne fairly freely.

I. I. A. MYRTIFOLIA AUREO-MACULATA B, 2. I. A. SERRATIFOLIA AUREO-
MACULATA, 3. I. A. AUREA MARGINATA ANGUSTIFOLIA, 4. I. A. AUREA-
MARGINATA BROMELIÆFOLIA, 5. I. A. AUREA MARGINATA OVATA,
6. I. A. AUREA MARGINATA STRICTA

Reproduced by permission of the Editor of " The Gardeners' Chronicle "

I. Aquifolium Varieties

I. A. aurea marginata crispa = crispa marginata.—This is one of the many forms of aurea marginata and is not very distinct. Mr Moore describes it as bearing considerable resemblance to I. A. aurea marginata intermedia in size and form of leaf, but the leaf is of an opaque green, and the edge is unequally bordered with dull yellow; it is also very much divaricate the spines being often reduced. The bark of the young wood is brownish.

I. A. aurea marginata fructu-luteo = fructu-luteo aurea variegata, "Yellow-berried Variegated" and "Gold-striped Variegated."—This is a green barked variety with bold, ovate leaves, 2½ to 3 inches long, coarsely and rather distantly spined, the spines strongly divaricate. The colour of the disk is green, blotched with grey, the edge being greenish-yellow or yellow broken with green, not remarkable for clearness or distinctness of marking. Indeed, apart from its very distinct yellow fruit, it is, as a variegated shrub, not by any means an attractive sort.

I. A. aurea marginata intermedia = intermedia aurea marginata.—A neat golden Holly with brownish young bark, and ovate leaves. The largest of the latter are about 2 inches long and an inch broad, the disk dark green or mottled, the golden margin broadest at the tips and the spines broad and strongly developed. Mr Moore records a variety from Ochtertyre

Holly, Yew and Box

called I. A. rigida marginata similar to this except that it had green bark.

I. A. aurea marginata ovata.—This is a distinct variety with reddish brown young wood. The leaves are ovate, with strongly developed and tolerably regular spines; the disk is mottled green and grey and there is a broad pale yellow edge. The broad outline of the leaves and their strongly spiny margins, together with the amount of colouration, renders this a very desirable variety for ornamental plantations.

I. A. aurea marginata pallida.—A green-barked variety with ovate leaves, 2 to 2½ inches long, and weak and irregular spines. The disk is mottled green, the border greenish-yellow and narrow at the base merging into a broad yellow border at the apex.

I. A. aurea marginata salicifolia = salicifolium foliis aureis marginatis.—A curious, dwarf, slow growing Holly with every small, lanceolate leaves about an inch long and ¼ to ⅓ of an inch wide. The disk is green streaked with a few lines of grey, the spines and narrow border being pale yellow, while the whole tip of the leaf and frequently half the surface is also yellow. The bark of the young shoots is purplish. It is very distinct from other varieties.

I. A. aurea marginata stricta = stricta aurea marginata.—This variety belongs to the purple barked series. The leaves are oblong or elliptic,

I. Aquifolium Varieties

2½ to 3 inches long, of a dark green colour with broad streaks of grey running parallel to the veins, and with a definite and tolerably regular edge of pale straw-yellow. The spines are bold but irregular, and lie in the plane of the leaf, and they appear always to stop more or less short of the base.

I. A. aurea regina = "Golden Queen."—This is a beautiful Holly and certainly the best of the golden variegated series. The bark of the young wood is green, and the leaves are broadly ovate, 2½ inches to 3½ inches long, and 1½ to 2 inches broad, with very strong, spreading and variously directed spines. The disk is usually much mottled with dark green, pale green and grey, often in nearly equal proportions, and there is a broad, well defined, continuous margin of deep golden yellow. It is a free growing but sterile variety. The tendency to variegation is so strongly marked on this beautiful plant that it is not uncommon—notwithstanding its robust habit of growth—to find leaves which, either on one side of the mid-rib, or both, are entirely gold coloured. On different plants a difference of shade in the golden colouring can sometimes be detected. It forms a very useful plant for a lawn specimen and no collection should be without it.

I. A. aurea regina nigra.—A variety bearing a strong resemblance to the true "Golden Queen" on one hand and I. A. aurea marginata

Holly, Yew and Box

latifolia on the other. It differs from "Golden Queen" by having the bark of the young wood of a reddish purple hue very similar to that of aurea marginata latifolia. The leaves are fully as large as those of "Golden Queen" and very similar in shape, the spines being very strong and divaricate. The disk is dark green, blotched with grey green, the margin golden and irregular in outline usually narrower than that of "Golden Queen." It is a female variety and in this resembles the large-leaved golden-edged form.

I. A. aurea regina pendula = "Gold Weeping" and pendula aurea marginata.—A fine weeping, golden variegated Holly belonging to the purple-barked section. The leaves are about 2½ inches long by 1½ inches wide, ovate, or oblong-ovate, very strongly divaricate, the spines being stout, tolerably equal in size, and set at moderate distances though occasionally widely separated. The disk is conspicuously mottled with yellowish or greyish green on a dark green ground and the yellow margin, though irregular, is well marked and broadish, sometimes extending half way across the leaf. Mr Moore kept the two names aurea pendula and aurea regina pendula as distinct varieties owing to a slight difference in the spinyness of the leaves.

I. A. aurifodina = aurifodina marginata, croceofuscum, aureum scoticum, and "Smudge Holly." These names according to Moore represent the

1. I. A. AUREA REGINA, 2. I. A. AURIFODINA, 3. I. A. COOKII,
4. I. A. AUREA REGINA PENDULA
Reproduced by permission of the Editor of " The Gardeners' Chronicle"

I. Aquifolium Varieties

same plant which is strikingly distinct and handsome, especially during the winter months. The bark is usually reddish, but occasionally green. The leaves are ovate-acuminate, about 1¾ inches long, the spines continuous but distant, placed along the edge, or rarely few and scattered, moderately divaricate, the disk dark green, flushed or marbled with dull yellow green, the edge unequally marked with tawny orange yellow, sometimes extending over fully half of the leaf. It is of upright or pyramidal habit, thickly clothed with the medium-sized or rather small foliage, and very distinct and peculiar on account of the tawny hue which the variegation assumes during the winter season.

I. A. Cookii = obscura.—A neat looking purple-barked Holly, the leaves of which are broadly ovate, flat, and furnished with even, moderate sized spines. The disk is dark green mottled-with grey and yellowish green the margin being of the latter colour and narrow. Occasionally whole leaves may be found green or yellow. It is a female variety and not very ornamental though distinct.

I. A. heterophylla aureo marginata = lævigata, " Striped Bay-leaved," Egham Holly and Old Gold."—A very striking and distinct green-barked Holly with two distinct types of leaf. One type is similar in form to an ordinary spiny leaf of Common Holly with the addition of

Holly, Yew and Box

a golden edge. Leaves of this type vary from 2 to 3 inches in length and from 1 to 1½ inches in width with wavy margins armed with numerous, strong, divaricate spines. The disk is deep green, splashed with grey and yellow, the whole being edged with an irregular golden margin. The other form of leaf is usually from 2½ to 4 inches long, by 1¾ to 2 inches broad, with the spines very few in number, entirely absent, or represented by a terminal one only. What spines are borne are strong and erratically placed. The disk is dark glossy green heavily splashed with greenish yellow and margined with the same. Sometimes quite half the leaf is yellow whilst at others it is reduced to a narrow but irregular border. It closely resembles heterophylla aureo-picta but the latter rarely has the variegation extending to the margins of the leaves.

I. A. laurifolia aurea = aureum mucronatum, aurea longifolia and "Striped laurifolia."—This variety has usually purplish or reddish brown bark, but sometimes greenish, and elliptic-ovate or ovate leaves from 2 to 2½ inches long, slightly wavy on the margin, sometimes entirely, usually almost spineless, occasionally with two to four erratic spines on each side, dark glossy green, with indistinct patches of paler green, and with a narrow edge of bright, golden yellow.

I. A. "Madame Briot."—A distinct purple-barked variety of continental origin, with oblong-

I. Aquifolium Varieties

ovate leaves 2½ to 3 inches long and 1¼ to 1½ inches wide, armed on the margins with strongly developed, divaricate spines. The surface is mottled with yellow and green on the disk and there is a golden margin which varies considerably in width sometimes being reduced to a mere line whilst at others it extends almost to the mid-rib. Occasionally whole leaves assume a rich golden colour. It is a very effective and ornamental variety.

I. A. muricata = bicolor.—This is a green-barked variety with ovate or oblong-ovate, acuminate leaves which vary from 1¾ to 2½ inches in length and from ¾ to 1 inch in breadth. The leaves are moderately flat and spiny, the spines being short and fairly evenly distributed along the margins, the majority pointing in one direction. The disk is dark green, heavily streaked or blotched with grey or greenish yellow, the marginal band being of irregular width, generally widening about the apex, and yellow tinged with green. Mr Moore kept "bicolor" as a distinct variety, saying that it was near "muricata." I have however failed to detect sufficient variation to warrant the two names being kept up.

I. A. myrtifolia aurea = myrtifolia aureo-marginata, striped serratifolia, pectinata aureo-marginata.—This is a distinct golden Holly with small glossy leaves and purple bark. The leaves are lanceolate or ovate-lanceolate, about 1½ to 2

113

inches long, with unequal and irregular spines, which are sometimes a good deal divaricated, and at other times nearly plane ; they have a disk of dark mottled green, the central parts being freely marked with grey and yellow-green, while the edge, which is of a pale golden yellow, is often broad and usually well defined, though occasionally running in on broadish patches. It is one of the best small-leaved golden forms.

I. A. myrtifolia elegans = serrata elegans marginata and "De Smet's Holly."—A narrow-leaved golden-edged form with reddish-brown bark. The leaves are lanceolate, 1½ inches long, with rather distant and distinct spines, which are somewhat wavy ; the ordinary colour is a greenish centre with a narrowish golden edge, but the leaves are sometimes either partially or wholly golden.

I. A. repanda.—A peculiar-looking green-barked variety, with broadly ovate leaves, 2¾ to 3 inches long, sometimes almost entire, sometimes broadest towards the apex, usually with a sinuate or repand margin, the projecting parts of which occasionally terminate in a short imperfect angular tooth, these teeth being distant and unequally placed. The surface is dark green, slightly mottled, and bordered with a nearly obsolete yellow margin.

I. A. rubricaulis aurea.—This is a variety with rather short but wide leaves, peculiar for its reddish brown bark, leaf stalks, and red tinged

I. Aquifolium Varieties

spines. The leaves are 1½ to 2 inches long and about 1 inch wide. In some instances the spines are very strong and divaricate, in others small and mostly pointing in one direction; the colour is deep green with a faint yellow margin, the spines being the same colour but tinged with red. In all cases the spines are numerous. It is a fruiting variety.

I. A. scotica aurea = "Striped Scotica," and scotica aurea superba.—A beautiful dwarf-growing Holly, with purple bark. The leaves are about 1½ inches long, obovate, marginate, nearly entire but loosely wavy, narrowing to wedge-shape at the base; the disk dark mottled green, with a broad golden edge, most developed towards the apex. Mr Moore thought the form he called superba was distinct, but it had only just originated when he described it, and it has not been kept separate.

I. A. speciosa.—This is a green-barked variety with the leaves below medium size, being 1¾ inches in length; they are of an ovate form, with a conspicuously mottled centre, and a deep golden edge.

I. A. "Victoria."—This is an ornamental variety with medium-sized leaves, bearing strong, evenly developed divaricate spines. The bark is red as also are the leaf-stalks when young. The leaves are oblong, 2 to 2½ inches long and 1 inch wide, the disk green with paler markings, surrounded

Holly, Yew and Box

with a moderately wide golden margin most conspicuously developed about the apex, whilst sometimes whole branches develop golden leaves with no trace of green.

I. A. walthamensis.—A variety with very strongly developed spines for the size of the leaf, which is only about 1½ inches in length. It is of elliptic form with the spines much divaricated. The disk is mottled and streaked with yellowish green, and it has a broad and conspicuous yellow margin. The bark of the young shoots is reddish brown.

I. A. Watereriana = "Waterer's Gold," "Waterer's Gold-striped," nana aurea variegata, aureum pumilum, and compacta aurea.—This is one of the most distinct and easily recognised of the numerous golden variegated Hollies, and in addition one of the most ornamental. It is specially adapted for a position where a close, neat, slow-growing variety is required, being naturally compact, slow-growing and dense, needing very little pruning. It is very rarely that a really vigorous leading shoot is formed. The bark of the young shoots is green, striped with greenish yellow. The leaves vary in shape and size, and may be either oblong, ovate or obovate, and often oblique. They measure from 1½ to 2½ inches in length, and from 1 to 1⅓ inches in width. The spines are usually few in number, and produced at irregular intervals, and are never strongly developed.

1 & 2. I. A. LAURIFOLIA AUREA, 3. I. A. MYRTIFOLIA AUREA,
4. I. A. LAURIFOLIA SULPHUREA, 5. I. A. WATERERIANA
Reproduced by permission of the Editor of " The Gardeners' Chronicle"

I. Aquifolium Varieties

Occasionally the spines are absent except for a small terminal one, whilst more frequently they are represented by from two to six on the upper half of the leaf. The disk of the leaf is dark green, mottled often in sectional streaks with yellowish green and greyish green, and there is a broad but irregular marginal band of deep golden-yellow, which is not continuous; not unfrequently they are wholly golden or half golden. It is an exceptionally good plant for the formal garden, as it grows into a compact shape without having to be made hideous by clipping.

I. A. angustifolia aurea maculata.—A variety with leaves similar in size and shape to those of angustifolia, but having the disks unevenly marked with gold. It closely resembles myrtifolia aureo-maculata.

I. A. aurea marginata latifolia.—This is a purple-barked variety which bears a striking resemblance to aurea regina nigra. The leaves are ovate, 2 to 2½ inches long, strongly divaricate, and with strongly developed spines. The disk is splashed with pale green, and there is an irregular deep golden edge. It is a fruiting sort.

XIV

OTHER EVERGREEN HOLLIES

I. **CASSINE,** *Walters* = I. vomitaria, I. religiosa, and Cassine caroliniana. Commonly called " Cassena."—This is one of the least ornamental of the hardy evergreen Hollies, and it is not grown in gardens to any great extent. It is found in the Southern United States, being specially abundant in swamps and rich moist soil in Florida, Carolina and Virginia, where it forms a bush or small tree 12 to 30 feet in height. The leaves are small, dark green and glabrous, with crenate or serrate margins. White flowers are produced in June, which are followed by red fruits. It is reported to have been considered a holy tree by many of the southern tribes of American Indians, who used it during their religious rites and councils. The various tribes are stated to have made pilgrimages to places where it grew abundantly, for the purpose of collecting the leaves and branches which were boiled, and the liquid drunk several days in succession for medicinal purposes. It is probably on this account that the names of I. vomitaria and I.

GROUP OF JAPANESE HOLLIES
1. ILEX INTEGRA, 2. I. LATIFOLIA, 3. I. SIEBOLDI, 4. I. CRENATA
5. I. CRENATA MARIESII, 6. I. CRENATA MAJOR, 7. I. CRENATA
VARIEGATA
All much reduced

Other Evergreen Hollies

religiosa have been given to the plant. I. Cassine was introduced to English gardens in 1700, and is sometimes called the "South Sea Tea."

I. cornuta, *Lindley and Paxton* = "Horned Holly."—Although this is one of the most curious and interesting of the hardy species, and at the same time a very ornamental Holly, it is still very uncommon in gardens, though it was introduced upwards of half a century ago. It was first brought to notice by Robert Fortune in 1846, who discovered it in April of that year in the neighbourhood of Shanghæ when collecting for the Horticultural Society. Greater prominence was given to it three years later, when it was put into commerce by Messrs Standish & Noble of Bagshot; and a year later, 1850, a good figure of it was given in *Paxton's Flower Garden, Vol. I. p.* 43. This was followed shortly after by figures and descriptions in the *Gardener's Chronicle* for 1850, *p.* 311, and in *Moore and Ayre's Magazine, Vol. II. p.* 277, *f.* 3. In 1858 it was figured in the *Botanical Magazine, t.* 5059.

Collectors of more recent dates than Fortune have found it in various parts of China, Dr A. Henry and Mr E. H. Wilson reporting it as growing in Ichang and the immediate neighbourhood, and cultivated in low lying districts.

When mature, it forms a low, bushy-headed

Holly, Yew and Box

tree with very curious, thick, leathery, glossy
leaves of a yellowish green hue above and pale
beneath. In shape, the leaves are very peculiar,
reminding one somewhat of an oblong sail with
the sides bellying in with the wind, or a square-
bottomed kite. Each leaf has usually five spines,
which are strong and sharp. Two of these appear
at the base, and three at the apex arranged in a
horn-like manner, which has given rise to the
common name of " Horned-Holly." The margins
of the leaves are very thick in texture, revolute,
and sometimes produce here and there additional
tiny spines which have an inward tendency.
From a fruiting specimen in the Kew Herbarium,
collected by Fortune in 1846, it appears that the
upper leaves on mature trees vary in shape,
sometimes being spineless and sometimes bearing
but one or two spines. The flowers are white
and borne in axillary clusters in April. They are
succeeded by bright red fruits, each of which
terminates a slender stalk half an inch long.
The bark, when young, is of a bright, yellowish
green; when older it is marked with brown.
Lindley and Paxton are responsible for the name.
A description of it has been published under the
name of I. furcata.

I. **crenata,** *Thunberg.*—The collector Maximowicz, who collected between 1860 and
1864, and who was one of the pioneers among
European explorers in Japan, is credited with

Other Evergreen Hollies

being the first to introduce living plants of this species into Europe. In 1864 he is stated to have sent live plants of this and I. integra to the St Petersburg Botanic Garden.

Professor Sargent in his *Forest Flora of Japan* describes it as being the most widely distributed and most common of Japanese Hollies, being met with in all parts of the Empire, either wild or cultivated, sometimes as small shrubs 3 to 4 feet high, and again, under cultivation, as small trees 20 feet in height. At the foot of Mount Hakkodo, an extinct volcano, it is said to be abundant, growing in company with I. Sugeroki and I. integra var. leucoclada. It is cultivated largely throughout Japan, and is used for dwarfing and cutting into fantastic shapes.

Under cultivation in Britain it is found to be of slow growth, but forms a very neat, compact, evergreen bush, usually 2 to 4 feet high, but sometimes upwards of 10 feet, and the same through. The leaves are Box-like, very small, ovate, with margins crenate and slightly revolute, in colour dark green. The stipules are larger than in most Hollies. The flowers are whitish and the fruits black. From herbarium specimens some difference is found to exist in the size of the leaves on different plants, those of some being almost an inch long, and wide in comparison, while those of others are scarcely half that size. A variety known as I. c. major is in

Holly, Yew and Box

cultivation ; it has very wide leaves, and has been called I. Fortunei. Another ornamental variety is I. c. variegata, a form with golden variegated leaves. I. c. Mariesii is a very distinct, slow-growing variety. It has roundish leaves, and a very stiff habit with crowded foliage.

Figures of I. crenata and varieties are given in *Lœsener's Monographia Aquifoliacearum, t.* 4, *f.* 2.

In the Coombe Wood nursery of Messrs Veitch a new Chinese plant is to be seen which bears a striking resemblance to a strong growing plant of I. crenata. It however differs by its looser and more vigorous habit, larger and rounder, glossier leaves, prominent buds, very pubescent branches and very minute stipules. The stipules are distinctly different, those in the present plant being mere dots whilst those of I. crenata are large for the genus. It will probably turn out to be I. yunnanensis, *Franchet*, or a form of that species. See illustration in group of new Chinese species.

I. corallina, *Franchet.*—At first sight this species bears some resemblance to I. Aquifolium chinensis ; it, however, differs by having larger leaves with curiously arranged spines, the latter pointing in several distinct directions, some being turned back in a rather curious manner. The leaves are evergreen, 4 to 6 inches long by 1 to 1½ inches wide with an acuminate apex. Both branches and leaves have a very smooth appearance. The tiny fruits are red and borne in small clusters. It is found in the province of Hupeh, and is not in general cultivation.

I. Dahoon, *Walters* = " The Dahoon Holly," I. cassinoides and I. laurifolia, *Link.* not *Hort.*—I. Aquifolium var. scotica is sometimes met with under the name of I. Dahoon, but it is an entirely different plant. I. Dahoon is a native of the S. United States, and it is doubtful whether it is in cultivation now in English gardens. Loudon describes it as "a beautiful evergreen shrub or low tree with lanceolately elliptical, nearly entire leaves almost revolute in the margin ; the midrib, petiole, and branchlets villous. Flowers disposed in corymbose panicles, that are upon lateral and terminal peduncles, white, borne in May and June and followed by red fruits which ripen in December." It is stated to have been introduced in 1726.

I. dipyrena, *Wallich* = "Himalayan Holly." —This is an ornamental, Himalayan species of distinct appearance, and perfectly hardy in the neighbourhood of London. At Kew, a fine shapely specimen may be seen in the Holly collection, which measures 22 feet high and 16 feet through. Sir D. Brandis, in his *Forest Flora of N. W. and Central India*, states that "it is common in the Himalaya from the Hindus to Bhotan at elevations varying from 5,000 to 9,000 feet." It there forms a straight symmetrical trunk 30 to 40 feet high with a large girth, one being recorded near Naini-Tal with a circumference of 16 or 17 feet. The branches are said to form a dense oval crown. The leaves vary considerably in size and spininess, the average being about 4½ inches in length and 1 inch in width. They are evergreen, dull in appearance, and edged with spiny teeth which vary considerably in length, sometimes being quite tiny and at others long and sharp. As the trees age spines often disappear as in the "Common Holly." The fruits are borne on stout foot stalks ⅓ of an inch long, are large, red and oval, and often contain but two seeds, though this is not a definite character as quite frequently more are produced. The young wood is distinct in character, being rather prominently too angled and twisted. The axillary buds are very different in appearance from those of other hardy Hollies, being very prominent and rounded, those of most of the better known Hollies being acuminate. The flowering period is two or three weeks in advance of that of the "Common Holly." Good examples are to be found at Leonardslee, Osborne, Kew and Abbotsbury.

I. d. elliptica = I. A. elliptica and I. A. flammea angustifolia.—Though usually included as a variety of I. Aquifolium, this is undoubtedly a form of I. dipyrena, wood, buds, leaves and fruit agreeing in every particular, whilst the flowering period is in

ILEX DIPYRENA IN THE ROYAL GARDENS, KEW

Other Evergreen Hollies

advance of the " Common Holly." It is a female form, and fruits are borne quite freely ; the percentage of fertile seeds borne by specimens removed a short distance from a male plant of the same species is however small. The varietal name is given on account of the leaves being elliptic in form.

I. Fargesii, *Franchet* = This is a curious species from Western China, remarkable for its long narrow leaves. It is stated to grow to a height of 15 feet in China. The branches are thin, and the bark glossy and of a reddish hue. The leaves are evergreen, 3 to 4 inches long and ¼ to ⅓ of an inch wide, with slightly serrated margins, deep green above and paler beneath. The apex is acuminate, the leaf stalks reddish. Fruits are borne in small axillary clusters, and are red in colour. Plants of this or a closely allied species are in cultivation at Coombe Wood, as yet however they are but of low stature.

I. insignis, *Hooker.*—For the warmer parts of the country such as Cornwall and South Wales, this handsome Himalayan Holly is well adapted, though in colder parts it is doubtful whether it could be successfully grown out-of-doors. It has been collected in Sikkim at an elevation of 7000 feet, and it is there stated to form a moderate-sized tree. The branches in a young state are sometimes of a reddish brown hue, and at others have a glaucous appearance.

Holly, Yew and Box

The oblong, acuminate leaves are handsome, evergreen, and often from 7 to 9½ inches long and 3 inches wide. The margins are armed with spines, which in some cases are very pronounced, and in others reduced to a mere serration. The mid ribs and principal veins are very well defined. The fruits are large, scarlet and sessile.

I. **integra**, *Thunberg*.—Under the name of Othera japonica this Chinese and Japanese species is occasionally met with in gardens. It is recognised by means of its pyramidal, or somewhat fastigiate habit, and its usually quite entire, dark green foliage.

In Japan it is stated to attain a height of 30 or 40 feet, and to be a favourite subject for cultivation in gardens attached to temples. The leaves are generally from 3 to 4 inches long, with petioles ½ to ¾ of an inch in length. They are thinner in texture than those of the "Common Holly," more or less ovate in shape, very dark green above, and pale green beneath. Although usually flat, with entire margins, the edges sometimes assume a wavy character, and occasionally a tendency to rudimentary spines or serration is noticeable. The flowers are white and borne during late spring. The fruits are bright red when ripe and vary greatly in size, the larger ones being nearly ½ an inch in diameter. They ripen in late autumn, and are very showy. Living plants were introduced to Europe in 1864.

Other Evergreen Hollies

Its distribution is wide, and it has been collected in many places. Between 1853 and 1856 Mr C. Wright gathered specimens in the Loo Choo Islands; in 1859 Coll. C. Wilford found it in Corea and so on. In 1862 Mr R. Oldham collected a dwarf form with small, oval leaves, in Nagasaki in Japan. A variety exists with yellow fruits called I. integra var. leucoclada. Good specimens of this, collected by the Rev. Pére Faurie in 1889, are included in the collections in the Kew Herbarium. *Professor Sargent*, in his *Forest Flora of Japan*, says that he saw this variety growing at the foot of Mount Hakkoda with I. crenata and I. Sugeroki.

When young I. integra is a rather slow grower and a little tender, so it is not advisable to plant it in very exposed places. It has been known under the names of I. Aquifolium var. Bessoni and I. integrifolia. The latter name must not be confused with I. A. var. integrifolia, which is quite another plant.

I. **latifolia**, *Thunberg* = magnoliæfolia, Tarajo and " Magnolia-leaved Holly."—In the *Garden and Forest* for March 1893 Professor Sargent describes this as being " probably the handsomest evergreen tree that grows in Japan." Unfortunately it is somewhat tender, and only grows successively in the warmer parts of our Isles. At Kew it has lived our-of-doors for many years, but growth is very slow. When

Holly, Yew and Box

at its best it forms a striking plant, the leaves being bold and handsome, whilst the fruit is ornamental.

Described by Thunberg, it was first introduced to Europe by Dr Siebold, who sent it to Belgium in 1840. A year later Mr Joseph Knight of the Exotic Nursery, Chelsea, obtained plants, and in 1852 a description and figure of it appeared in the third volume of *Paxton's Flower Garden*, *p. 13, fig.* 240. In the same year a similar description and figure was produced in the *Gardener's Chronicle*, whilst subsequently it was made the subject of a plate in the *Botanical Magazine, t.* 5597.

It is only found in the southern parts of Japan, and it there grows to a height of 50 to 60 feet. The leaves are ovate and serrate, and vary much in size, some being but about 4 inches long by 2 inches wide, whilst others are more than double those dimensions. The depth of serration differs, but in no case do the margins become spiny. The flowers are yellowish green, and are succeeded by large quantities of bright red fruits.

In the *Gardener's Chronicle* for 1866, *p.* 1046, an account is given of its flowering in the Temperate House at Kew. This was probably the first time it blossomed in this country.

Good-sized specimens which fruit well are to be found in the garden of Sir Edmund Loder at Leonardslee, one particular specimen being 20

Other Evergreen Hollies

feet high and 10 feet through, at Osborne and at Abbotsbury Castle.

I. opaca, *Aiton.*—In America this occupies the same position that the "Common Holly" does in Europe, and is known under the common names of "American Holly" and "Opaque-leaved Holly." It is widely distributed through the southern and eastern states, New York being given as its most northern and eastern limit. It is said to be very common in Carolina, Georgia, Louisiana, Arkansas, Texas, and Florida, reaching its largest dimensions in the dry Oak woods of Florida, and, according to Sargent, on the bottom lands of streams in S. Arkansas and E. Texas. It is put to much the same uses in America as the "Common Holly" is in England, *i.e.* ornamental planting, hedges, etc., whilst its economic properties are very similar.

Under favourable conditions it attains a height of 40 to 45 feet, with a trunk 24 to 36 inches in diameter, but is more frequently met with in a smaller state. The leaves are evergreen, very dull in colour, and vary considerably in size ; the larger ones are from 4 to 4½ inches in length, and 1½ to 1¾ inches in width. The margins are spiny, but the spines are less ferocious than those of I. Aquifolium. On old specimens the upper leaves are sometimes destitute of spines. The flowers are whitish, and succeeded by numerous small, coral red fruits, a well fruited example

Holly, Yew and Box

being quite as showy as the "Common Holly."
It does not appear to have produced many
varieties, though there is one with yellow fruit,
but it is quite probable that hybrids between it
and I. Aquifolium have originated, for the two
species have been growing side by side since
I. opaca was brought from America in 1744.
Here and there throughout the country large
specimens are met with. The largest one at
Kew at the present time is 23 feet high and 17
feet through.

I. pedunculosa, *Miquel.*—A native of China and
Japan, but it is doubtful whether it is in cultivation in this country. In Professor Sargent's
description he says that it has entire, oval or
ovate-acuminate leaves, with solitary fruits,
terminating long slender stalks, the fruits being
about the size of those of the "Common Holly."
Herbarium specimens show some variation, however, in size of fruit, whilst Chinese specimens
collected by Dr A. Henry show leaves, 3 to 4
inches long by 1½ inches wide with slight
signs of serration. It varies considerably in
size, sometimes being found as a shrub 2 to 3
feet high, and at other times as a large bush 20
to 30 feet in height.

I. Perado, *Aiton.*—Although at Kew this plant
is cultivated in the Temperate House, it is
quite probable that it will stand out-of-doors in
many parts of the country. Loudon mentions

GROUP OF NEW CHINESE HOLLIES FROM THE NURSERY OF MESSRS.
VEITCH OF CHELSEA

1. I. FARGESII, 2. I. AQUIFOLIUM CHINENSIS, 3. I. PERNYI,
4. I. PERNYI VAR., 5. I. SPECIES, 6. I. AFF. TO I. CRENATA,
7. I. CORALLINA
All much reduced

it as being hardy in the Horticultural Society's garden, and as having stood the winter of 1837-8. It forms a moderate-sized tree, with oval leaves which are often blunt at the apex. They vary considerably in size, sometimes attaining a length of 6 inches and a width of 3 to 4 inches, or again they may be little more than half that size. They are dark green in colour, often entire, but sometimes have the margins armed with short, spiny teeth. The fruits are large, deep red, or sometimes almost black, and borne in dense axillary clusters. It is quite likely that it has been used as a parent in the production of some of the garden Hollies. Madeira is given as its home, but it is also found in N. Africa. The date of its introduction to English gardens is said to have been 1760, the introducer being a Mr James Gordon.

I. Pernyi, *Franchet.* — This is without doubt one of the most interesting of the hardy evergreen species. It was named in honour of the French Missionary, Paul Perny, of the Missions Etrangeres Provicaire apostolique in Kuichou 1850 to 1860. He was the first botanical and zoological explorer of the province of Kuichou, and his first entry to the province was in the disguise of a Chinese beggar. The species was first described by M. Franchet upwards of twenty years ago, and in 1886 a figure and description appeared in *Hooker's Icones Plantarum, t.* 1539.

Holly, Yew and Box

Specimens showing both fruit and leaves were collected by Dr Augustine Henry in Patung and also in the province of Hupeh, Central China. It was however left to Mr E. H. Wilson when collecting in Central China for Messrs Veitch to send home seeds from which plants, now in Messrs Veitch's Nursery at Coombe Wood, were raised.

When mature, I. Pernyi usually forms a bush anything from 6 to 12 or 15 feet high; but according to Dr Henry, when growing under favourable conditions it sometimes attains a height of 30 feet. Under cultivation it has so far proved to be a rather slow grower, of bushy habit and dense leafage. The type is recognised by its small, deep green, glossy, coriaceous leaves which are from 1 to 1½ inches long with recurved margins and strong divaricate spines, the upper side being deep green, the under surface of quite a pale shade. The spines are from five to seven in number, the lower ones short, the upper ones long, the terminal one being lengthened out into an acuminate point, the whole being arranged in a similar manner to those of I. cornuta, in fact the whole leaf bears a striking resemblance to a diminutive form of that species. The fruits are the size of those of the smallest forms of the "Common Holly," red, sessile on the branches and borne in the leaf axils. If pulled off the branches a leaf is usually detached at the same time.

Other Evergreen Hollies

Among the seedlings at Coombe Wood a considerable variation in habit is noticeable. By the kindness of Messrs Veitch, we are enabled to give illustrations of the type and the most extreme form. The latter is recognised by its less dense foliage, broadly-ovate, flattened leaves, nearly 2 inches long and an inch wide, small spines all pointing in one direction and margins but very slightly revolute. The buds are very prominently developed and the leaf stalks are shorter than those of the type. Compared with typical Pernyi it looks distinct enough for specific rank, but intermediate forms are to be seen at Coombe Wood, in fact, some fit closely a variety in the Kew Herbarium called I. P. manipurensis, which was collected by Sir George Watt during the Government Demarcation Survey in Manipur in 1882.

I. **Sugeroki**, *Maximowicz.* — This is not in general cultivation, but is described in *Sargent's Forest Flora of Japan* as very handsome in autumn. In this work it is described as a spreading bush 5 to 6 feet high with stout branchlets, light green, ovate leaves, 1 inch long, rounded at the apex, coarsely crenulated above the middle, and bright scarlet, solitary, long stalked fruits.

XV

I. PLATYPHYLLA

Description

I. PLATYPHYLLA, *Webb and Berthelot* = I. A. platyphylla, *Hort.* — The set of large leaved, garden Hollies typified by this plant are essentially different from the varieties of I. Aquifolium, under which species they are usually included. Without doubt some of the sorts that approach the type in appearance are hybrids, and I. platyphylla and the "Common Holly" doubtless cross readily. A considerable amount of confusion exists in regard to the species, and many authorities make the garden I. platyphylla a variety of I. Aquifolium and keep it quite distinct from the Canary Island species. In every way, however, it agrees more closely with *Webb and Berthelot's* figure in *Phytographie Canariensis, II. pp.* 135-6, *t.* 68, with herbarium specimens collected in the Canary Islands, and with plants from Canary Island seeds, than with the "Common Holly." Moreover the large, broad leaved Hollies never produce typical "Common Holly" leaves, though the leaves may vary in size and form. I. platyphylla is doubtless

I AND 2. ILEX PLATYPHYLLA OF GARDENS.   3 AND 4. I. PLATY-
PHYLLA, W. AND B., TYPE.   5. I. PLATYPHYLLA NIGRESCENS
Much reduced

I. platyphylla

a variable plant, and is sometimes found wild
with leaves considerably larger than those of
cultivated plants in this country ; on the other
hand forms are met with, with foliage somewhat
smaller than that of our plant. Its nearest ally
appears to be I. Perado, and it approaches the
" Common Holly " most closely in the varieties
maderensis and balearica.

Occasionally met with under the name of the
" Broad-leaved Canary Island Holly," it has
been known to cultivation since 1760, though it
does not appear to have attracted any special
attention until many years later. In 1844 a
correspondent in the *Floricultural Cabinet* refers
to it as growing in a greenhouse at Kew and also
says that it grows freely in the open air and is
quite hardy in this country. It forms a handsome
evergreen tree of small stature, with large, dark
green, broadly oval leaves, often 4 to 5 inches
long and $2\frac{1}{4}$ to 3 inches wide, or occasionally on
wild plants 8 inches long and $4\frac{1}{2}$ inches wide,
with tiny, brown or black, triangular stipules.
The margins are usually unequally and irregularly
armed with short spines. Occasionally the spines
are wholly suppressed, but more frequently the
lower halves are spineless, whilst the upper
halves bear a few or many spines, and again the
margins are sometimes evenly armed with spines.
The apex is usually acute and terminated with
a spine, but this is not always the case. The

white flowers are borne in axillary cymes in May
and June, but the buds are very prominent the
previous autumn. When ripe, the fruits are deep
red, about $\frac{2}{7}$ of an inch in diameter with stout
foot stalks $\frac{1}{4}$ of an inch or so long, and are at
their best from October to February. During
the early stages of development the seeds are
deeply permeated with a reddish purple colouring matter. As in the case of the "Common
Holly," isolated plants perfect but a small percentage of seeds though to all outward appear-
ances fruits and seeds are fully matured. The
plant known in gardens as I. platyphylla is a
female or fruit-bearing plant, whilst there are
other named varieties whose principal difference
lies in the fact of their producing male flowers
only. The difference between some varieties
depends to a large extent on the shining or dull
surface of the leaves and by the degree of spininess. Seedlings differ somewhat in habit owing
no doubt to natural crossing, and some forms are
in commerce that it is difficult to ascribe to any
well marked variety, though they are not really
distinct enough for separate names. From seeds
collected from the large leaved varieties growing
away from "Common Holly" the difference
among the seedlings is not very pronounced.

SERIES OF LEAVES SHOWING TRANSITORY STAGES THROUGH WHICH
I. A. FEROX PASSES IN GETTING BACK TO TYPICAL I. AQUIFOLIUM.
THE LEAVES IN EACH CASE ARE FROM SINGLE PLANTS.

All much reduced

The numbering begins from the top left-hand corner

No 1. I. A. ferox, Nos. 2 to 8. I. A. Crispa, 5 and 6 are typical, whilst 2, 3 and 4 closely resemble
ferox, and 7 and 8 the next variety, scotica ; Nos. 9 to 12. I. A. scotica, 9 and 10 are typical whilst
11 and 12 approach the next variety, ovata ; Nos. 13 to 20. I. A. ovata. 15 and 16 are typical whilst
13 and 14 resemble some leaves of scotica and 17 to 20 show variations from ovata to typical
I. Aquifolium

1, 2 & 3. ILEX PLATYPHYLLA BALEARICA, 4, 5 & 6. I. PERADO, ·
7 & 8. I. SHEPHERDI, 9. I. "OAK VALE," 10 & 11. LEAVES
ATTACKED BY HOLLY FLY, "PHYTOMYZA ILICIS"

Numbering begins from the top left-hand corner
All much reduced

I. platyphylla

Varieties

I. p. balearica = **I. A. balearica.** — Although usually included as a variety of I. Aquifolium, this variety, from the Balearic Islands, is evidently a well-marked form of I. platyphylla, for, whilst it does not associate itself with any true form of "Common Holly" it has several features in common with platyphylla and closely resembles the variety maderensis. The habit is usually pyramidal and the leaves ovate or ovate-oblong, 3 to 3½ inches long and about 2 inches broad, thick in texture and bright green in colour. The majority of the leaves are entire or bear but a few erratically placed spines, though occasionally, short spines are fairly well represented along the margins. Its nearest affinity is maderensis and the general appearance of the two suggests that balearica is a female form of the same type of which maderensis is the male; herbarium specimens of this show great variation in character.

I. p. maderensis = I. A. maderensis, *Hort*, and I. maderensis. This is a very well marked variety with ovate or ovate-oblong leaves fairly regular in outline. The name maderensis was used by Lamarck in connection with another Canary Island plant, I. Perado : it is however quite distinct from the maderensis of gardens. The leaves of the plant under notice are usually 3 inches or rather more in length and about 1¾ to 2

137

inches broad, bright green, furnished throughout
the margin with tolerably regular spines lying in
the plane of the leaf and directed towards the
apex and rather stronger than those of platyphylla. The apex is acute and terminated with
a spine. It is a male form and grows into an
imposing specimen under favourable conditions.
For cold districts it is not so reliable as some
other sorts.

I. p. maderensis atrovirens = I. A. atrovirens
and I. A. maderensis atrovirens. — A form
which is considered to have darker leaves than
the type, but there is really no well marked
difference.

I. p. maderensis variegata = I. A. maderensis
variegata and I. A. maderensis picta.—A con-
picuous variety with reddish purple bark. The
leaves are ovate or obovate, rather smaller than
the type, about 2½ to 3 inches long and 1½ to 2¼
inches wide. The spines are evenly placed and
usually arranged in the same plane, though
occasionally a slight waviness is noticeable. The
margin is dark green with a feathered, golden
blotch mixed with pale green, in the centre. The
colours are bright and effective. It might readily
be taken to be of hybrid origin.

I. p. nigrescens = I. A. nigrescens. — A
distinct variety with ovate-oblong leaves, 3 to
3½ inches long and 2¼ to 2½ inches wide. The
apex is acute and the margin is often destitute

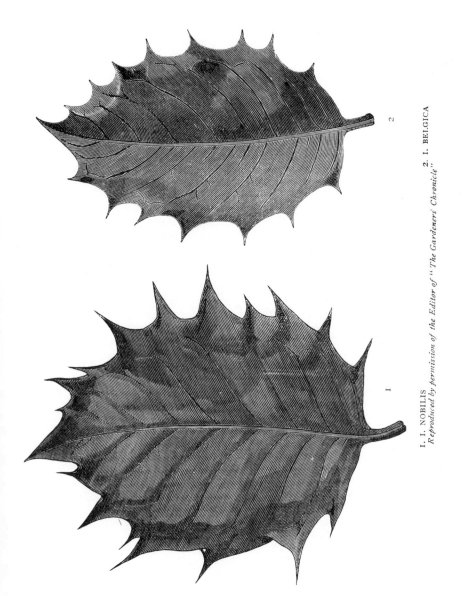

1. I. NOBILIS
Reproduced by permission of the Editor of "The Gardeners' Chronicle"

1. I. NOBILIS   2. I. BELGICA

I. platyphylla

of spines, though occasionally a few erratic ones are borne and at other times 4 or 5 pairs. In all instances they are small. The colour is brighter than that of the type and it forms a very vigorous specimen of ornamental character. It differs principally from the type in its comparatively spineless leaves and male flowers.

Broad-Leaved Hollies that are apparently of Hybrid Origin but approach Platyphylla most closely

I. altaclarensis = I. A. altaclarensis.—An exceptionally fine Holly with purplish bark, and large, deep green, roundish-ovate or oval leaves, 3 to 4 inches long, and 2½ to 3 inches wide, with stronger and more divaricate spines than I. platyphylla, which suggest some I. Aquifolium influence. On some leaves the spines are numerous and regularly developed, whilst on others they are few, or altogether absent. It is a male form of vigorous and dense habit, forming a noble specimen. The variety Hodginsii comes nearest to it in appearance.

I. belgica = I. A. belgica and "Dutch Holly."—A fine, vigorous habited variety, with the young bark green. The leaves are of a sapgreen, 3½ inches long, ovate, or oblong ovate, with a formidable array of strong and rather thickly-placed spines at the edge.

Holly, Yew and Box

I. Hendersoni = I. A. Hendersoni. — A distinct sort with green bark and opaque, dark green, oblong-elliptic leaves with sunken veins. They are from 2½ to 3½ inches long and from 1¾ to 2 inches wide. The apices are usually acute and the margins entire, or with a few small, scattered spines. It produces large fruits but not very freely.

I. Hodginsii = I. A. Hodginsii.—Several of the large leaved Hollies are so similar in appearance that it is difficult to fix on any distinguishing marks by which to identify them. Though some people declare that Hodginsii is really the same as Shepherdii, there are quite as many more who assert that the two plants are distinct. The probability is that one plant is a seedling from the other. Hodginsii, as usually known, comes near to altaclarensis, the leaves being darker in colour than those of Shepherdii. The leaves are dark green, roundish ovate, from 2¾ inches to 3¾ inches long, having bold marginal spines, somewhat distant but tolerably evenly disposed, or occasionally reduced to a few scattered ones only. It is a female variety of vigorous growth and very hardy.

I. Hodginsii aurea = I. A. Hodginsii aurea.— The leaves of this are of the broadly oval form of those of Hodginsii from which it is a sport. The disk is conspicuously mottled with dark and grey green, and there is a broad golden coloured

I. ALTACLARENSIS

Reproduced by permission of the Editor of " The Gardeners' Chronicle "

I. platyphylla

margin. It is of bold habit and very effective. Mr Moore records it as having been sent to him by the Lawson Nursery and Seed Company.

I. Hodginsii "King Edward VII."—This variety was put into commerce by Messrs Little and Ballantyne in 1898. It is a hardy and effective plant answering to the description of I. H. aurea, and it is possible that the plant Mr Moore describes under that name is the same variety, for it never seems to have become generally known as I. H. aurea. This variety was awarded a first class certificate by the Royal Horticultural Society.

I. Lawsoniana = I. A. Lawsoniana and Lawsoniana variegata.—This is really a variegated form of I. Hendersoni. It is a conspicuous sort, not only on account of the size of the leaves, but also for the bold and striking markings of their surface. It has the young bark of a reddish brown. The leaves ovate or bluntly elliptical, 2½ to 3½ inches long, the margins distantly but tolerably evenly spined and nearly or quite plane ; they are of an opaque green, the central or discal portions marked with broad bands or blotches of yellow, very variable in shape, but often occupying the greater part of the surface on one side the costa, the marginal portions green, showing two shades. Occasionally the spines are more numerous than in our figure (about 10 on each side), and sometimes

Holly, Yew and Box

less numerous when either the basal part or a portion of the side is spineless. It is one of the handsomest of the " Golden Hollies."

I. Mundyi.—This is a very distinct sort belonging to the green-barked set. It was sent out from the Handsworth Nurseries and is probably a natural hybrid with I. p. maderensis for one parent. The leaves are dull in appearance, regular in shape, broadly ovate and evenly spined along the whole of the margin, which is sometimes slightly undulated on one side. They are usually from 3 to 4 inches long, and 1½ to 2 inches wide, and are prominently and evenly veined, giving the upper side a somewhat ribbed appearance.

I. nobilis = I. Urquhartii. — This variety closely resembles altaclarensis, the leaves being dark green, roundish, and armed with bold spines ; for general purposes it is not distinct enough to warrant its being kept as a separate variety.

I. nobilis variegata is recognised by means of its golden variegated leaves, the variegation being confined to the centre with a broad green margin.

I. Shepherdii = I. A. Shepherdii. — This is one of the finest and hardiest of the large leaved Hollies. It was named in honour of Mr Shepherd the first Curator of the Liverpool Botanic Garden and was put into commerce by the Handsworth firm of nurserymen, It is a very vigorous sort

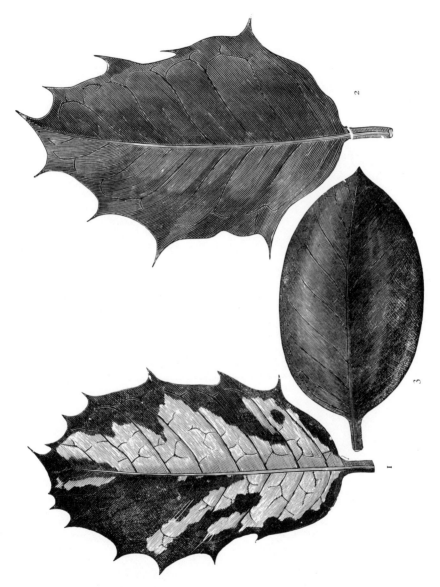

1. I. LAWSONIANA, 2. I. HODGINSII, 3. I. HENDERSONI
Reproduced by permission of the Editor of "The Gardeners' Chronicle"

1. ILEX MUNDYI, 2. I. AQUIFOLIUM ROBINSONIANUM, 3. I. A. MARNOCKI,
4. I. WILSONI, 5. I. A. LICHTENTHALII, 6. I. KING EDWARD VII,
7. I. PLATYPHYLLA MADERENSIS, 8 I. P. MADERENSIS VARIEGATA
All much reduced

I. platyphylla

with green bark. The leaves are stout in texture, from 2 to 3 inches or more long, broadly ovate with a short acumen, rarely quite spineless, occasionally few spined, or more frequently spiny throughout, with flat or plane, rather strongly developed spines which in rare instances become somewhat wavy or divaricate, indicating that it may possibly be of hybrid origin. Like most Hollies of this class the colour is rich; in this instance it is rather bright green, by which it is distinguishable from Hodginsii, which is of a much darker hue.

I. Wilsoni. — A vigorous growing, green-barked Holly belonging to the large leaved section. It is probably a natural hybrid and is one of the most ornamental of all the green leaved sorts. On healthy specimens the leaves grow to a large size, sometimes being upwards of 5 inches long, and 2½ inches wide. They are oval in form and are armed with numerous evenly developed spines a quarter of an inch or so long, which usually lie in the same plane and point in an upward direction. In shade they are dark, and they are very distinct by reason of the well-defined veins. It is a fruiting variety, the fruits being intermediate in size and colour between those of I. Aquifolium and I. platyphylla. When exhibited by the Handsworth firm in 1899 at a meeting of the Royal Horticultural Society, it was awarded a first class certificate.

XVI

THE DECIDUOUS HOLLIES

THE various N. American and Japanese species included under this heading constitute the group which have been given the special generic name of Prinos. The reason for this name being given was, that the parts of the flowers are usually found to be in sixes, whilst those of Ilex are in fours. Modern botanists, however, include all in Ilex.

I. ambigua, *Chapman.* — This N. American species is found about the sandy margins of swamps, forming a medium sized bush with pubescent branchlets and oval or oblong, acute or acuminate leaves with finely toothed margins. Occasionally the leaves are slightly pubescent, but more often smooth (*Chap. Fl. S. U. S.*). The sterile flowers are usually in clusters and the fertile ones solitary : the latter have also shorter petioles than the former.

I. **Amelanchier,** *Curtis* = Prinos lanceolata. — This is one of the representatives of the deciduous set of Hollies which have been called by a special generic name, *i.e.* Prinos. Being unacquainted

The Deciduous Hollies

with I. Amelanchier in a living state I have taken the following descriptive notes from *Chapman's Flora of the Southern United States.* "The leaves are oblong, 2 inches long and 1 inch wide, barely acute at each end, serrulate, pubescent and finely reticulate beneath; fruiting pedicels solitary, as long as the petioles; drupe large, red; nutlets strongly three-ribbed on the back, calyx teeth acute." Found as a large bush in swampy ground from Mississippi to N. Carolina.

I. decidua, *Walters* = I. æstivalis, I. prinoides, and Prinos deciduus.—A large growing deciduous shrub inhabiting swampy ground over a considerable area in the Southern United States. Under cultivation it forms a bush 12 to 15 feet high, and its principal attraction is its bright red berries which ripen in autumn. The leaves are from 1 to 2½ inches in length and half an inch to an inch wide, acuminate and gradually narrowing to a short petiole at the base. The margin is obtusely serrate and the upper surface is usually glabrous and glossy, the under surface being paler, with the mid-rib densely pubescent, and the secondary ones pubescent to a less degree. The flowers are small and white, and borne in axillary clusters on short pedicels. The female flowers are succeeded by small, bright red fruits, which ripen during late autumn.

I. glabra, *Gray* = Prinos glaber and "Ink-

Holly, Yew and Box

berry."—This is a semi-deciduous species, for although the leaves are often retained throughout winter it is not always so, and they always fall previous to new ones appearing. It is found in sandy soil near the coast from Massachusetts to Pennsylvania, Florida and Louisiana. Naturally a low growing bush, it is rarely met with more than 4 feet in height. The leaves are 1 to 1½ inches long, oblong or obovate with the margins near the apex slightly crenate, the lower portion being entire. The flowers are very tiny, the male ones being borne several together, whilst the female ones are usually solitary. The fruits are very small and black.

I. lævigata, *Gray* = Prinos lævigatus and " The Single Berry Black Alder." — This is one of the Prinos section which grows from 6 to 10 feet high and closely resembles I. verticillata from which it differs principally by its solitary, orange-scarlet fruit and longer pedicels. It is found in wet ground, and is widely distributed from Maine to Pennsylvania and from Georgia to Kentucky. The leaves are lanceolate or ovate and acuminate, with serrated margins. They are shining and glabrous on both surfaces except for a slight hairiness on the principal veins. The flowers are white and borne on stalks from ⅓ of an inch to an inch in length, and are succeeded by the orange scarlet fruits which ripen in autumn. In addition to the common name quoted above it is

The Deciduous Hollies

sometimes called the "Smooth-leaved Winter Berry."

I. macropoda, *Miquel.* — This is the largest growing of the Japanese deciduous Hollies. In Japan it is stated to form a round-headed tree 20 to 30 feet high, with a trunk sometimes as much as a foot in diameter. Its principal attraction from an ornamental standpoint lies in its bright red, long-stalked fruits.

I. rugosa, *F. Schmidt.*—This is a deciduous, Japanese species of little value for ornamental work. It forms a many-branched bush; a thicket of branches rising from one root-stock. The leaves are small, rugose, more or less ovate, with ciliate margins. The fruits are solitary in the leaf axils and are borne on long slender stalks. In comparison with other Hollies the flowers are rather large.

I. Sieboldi, *Miquel.* — This is very like the deciduous Hollies of N. America in general appearance. It cannot be called an ornamental plant by any stretch of imagination, except when covered with its red fruit in winter, and even then it is scarcely as bright as I. verticillata. A native of Japan, it forms a tall, spreading bush 12 feet or more high, with small, ovate, acute, serrate leaves. The flowers are small, borne in axillary clusters and are followed by tiny red berries. Berry-laden shoots are said to be sold in large quantities in Japanese towns for decorative purposes. It is found in damp ground about the margins of streams, etc., and varieties are met with bearing white and yellow fruits.

I. verticillata, *Gray* = Prinos verticillata, P. prunifolius, "Black Alder," "Winterberry" and "Fever Bush."—The latter three are the popular names under which the shrub is known in the United States. Under natural conditions it is found growing in swamps and low grounds from Nova Scotia to Ontario, Wisconsin, Florida, and Missouri, as a shrub from a few feet to 10 or 12 feet in height. The leaves are deciduous and show some considerable difference in size and shape. They are from $1\frac{1}{2}$ to 4 inches long and from $\frac{5}{8}$ of an inch to an inch wide, with petioles from $\frac{1}{3}$ of an inch to $\frac{1}{2}$ an inch long, and may be oval, obovate, or lanceolate in shape, with serrated margins, and sometimes rounded, but more often acuminate, apices. The undersides are downy. The flowers are white and six-parted, the male ones being borne several together in the leaf axils, the female ones being often borne singly but sometimes several together from axillary buds. The mature fruits are bright red, barely $\frac{1}{4}$ of an inch in diameter, and borne on short stalks no longer than the diameter of the fruit. The calyx lobes are retained until the fruit falls. There is a variety with yellow fruit.

In Woody Plants of Massachusetts we learn that "the bark and berries of the 'Black Alder' are

The Deciduous Hollies

somewhat bitter and astringent, and have been sometimes substituted for Peruvian bark in cases of intermittent fevers. The bark has also been considered of great use both taken internally and used as a wash in cases of incipient gangrene and eruptions of the skin."

This completes the descriptions of the hardy Hollies. We are aware that there are numerous other Hollies, more particularly forms of I. Aquifolium, not included in the foregoing descriptions, but as the majority are but seedlings or sub-varieties of the more distinct forms, they are hardly distinct enough for separate names.

THE YEW

XVII

THE YEW

THE various species of trees and shrubs which compose the genus Taxus are popularly known as Yews, and are included in the tribe Taxineæ of the large family Coniferæ. The hardy species are few in number, three only being of any importance for British gardens, whilst a fourth might be of value for the warmer parts of the British Isles, if it could be obtained in quantity.

The three commoner species are :

T. baccata, *Linnæus;* "The Common Yew."
T. canadensis, *Willdenow;* " The Canadian Yew."
T. cuspidata, *Siebold and Zuccarini;* " The Japanese Yew."

The more tender species is :

T. brevifolia, *Nuttall;* " The Californian Yew."

Between these species the distinguishing marks are not great, and some botanists consider that the number could well be reduced, and that T. canadensis and T. cuspidata might be included as geographical forms of T. baccata. Other scientists are in favour of making more species by giving specific rank to some of the distinct varieties of "Common Yew."

In old books the popular name of Yew is spelt in a variety of ways, some of the most common being, Yeugh, Eugh, Iw, Ewe, Yewgh, Ugh, and Yw. The last mentioned way is stated to be the Welsh method, whilst Iw is said to be Anglo-Saxon.

For both use and ornament, the Canadian, Japanese, and Californian Yews play but an insignificant part when compared with T. baccata, for, by many years of cultivation, selection of seedlings, natural sports, etc., a large number of varieties have been obtained, which are recognised by colour of foliage or habit, and these occupy an important place amongst evergreens for garden decoration.

T. baccata—Description

T. baccata is widely distributed through the greater part of Europe, except the extreme north and open plains of Russia, and extends across Asia eastwards of the Himalaya; it is also met with in Algeria. It is a common tree in the British Isles, and is fairly evenly dis-

The Yew

tributed, plants which must have originated as wild examples being met with in many different places, whilst ample evidence is at hand to prove that it formed at least a portion of the woods and forests of pre-historic times. In the Wood Museum at Kew pieces of Yew wood are preserved which were dug up from submerged forests in places so widely separated as Yorkshire and Somersetshire. The Yorkshire example was taken from beneath a bed of clay six feet in thickness on Hatfield Chase, near Thorne, and the Somersetshire specimen from a submarine forest near Stogursey. It is the patriarch of European trees, and in point of longevity holds its own with the giant Sequoias of California and Eucalyptuses of Australia. The oldest examples in Britain are usually found in the vicinity of churches, and numerous specimens exist whose ages are known to exceed one thousand years, whilst it is believed that the age of some almost doubles that number.

Although under cultivation, the Yew thrives in both full sun and dense shade, at sea level and at a medium elevation ; it is usually found in a state of nature in positions where it escapes the full power of the sun's rays, such as undergrowth amongst taller trees and the northern sides of hills and mountains. Its partiality to elevated ground, where it obtains some protection from scorching sun, is brought prominently into notice

Holly, Yew and Box

by its absence from the level plains of Russia, its habitat in that country being the mountainous regions of the Crimæa and Caucasus. It is usually described as a solitary tree, a description warranted by its being found singly or in small groups in woods or forests of other trees rather than composing woods or forests itself.

When allowed to grow naturally in open ground, it forms a many branched tree with a short, stout trunk and large head, and may be anything up to 40 or 50 feet in height. When growing amongst other trees, however, it is drawn up with a single trunk to a height of from 50 to 80 feet. Trees that have been drawn up in this manner, and are afterwards given light and space for development, form very handsome specimens, and it is quite probable that many of the fine old Yews now standing in isolated positions, have, at some earlier period of their existence, formed part of a wood. The timber of the Yew is very tough and durable, and, on account of its slow growth, very compact. It has been made use of by cabinet-makers and others, but all other uses are insignificant compared with its value in ancient times for the making of bows.

The bark is of a reddish-brown colour, and peels off annually in flakes, in a similar manner to the Plane-tree. The leaves are small, linear, flattened, and of a very deep shade of green, which, together with the density of the foliage,

The Yew

gives the trees, particularly old trees, a very sombre aspect. Although the species is usually diœcious, this is not always the case, for instances occur of both male and female flowers being borne by the same plant. The female flowers are very minute, and are not noticeable except under very close observation; the male blossoms, on the other hand, are rather conspicuous, for, though small, they are borne in such profusion as to be distinguishable from a considerable distance when ready to discharge their pollen during March or early April. Pollen is borne in such quantities as to discolour the ground beneath the trees when it is ripe, whilst on a windy day it leaves the trees in clouds. Both male and female flowers are borne from the leaf axils, and the latter are followed by small, nut-like seeds, enclosed, except for the tips, in bright red, fleshy cups. These seeds ripen from October to Christmas, and the bright cups are very effective, lighting up the dark foliage with pendants of coral. The Yews are dangerous trees to plant in places where cattle and other animals can get near enough to browse on them, for the leaves are poisonous, and many cases have been recorded of animals being killed by eating branches of Yew. The flowers and fruits were also regarded as poisonous at one time, and old writers warned apiarists against placing bee-hives in the neighbourhood of Yew trees, as,

Holly, Yew and Box

from the bees working the flowers, the honey would be sure to be poisonous. The fleshy cups of the seeds are certainly not poisonous—at any rate to birds and small boys, for both eat them greedily.

XVIII

T. BACCATA—*Continued*

Associations

THE extreme old age that the Yew attains, together with its slow growth, rugged aspect, sombre, melancholy appearance ; and its associations with churches and burial-grounds, has given rise to many curious legends, and these have been freely commented on by writers of both prose and verse. As in the case of those of the Holly, these legends are of very old standing, and are spoken of by some of our most ancient writers. Like the Holly, too, branches of the Yew have been made use of in connection with religious observances ; whilst, however, the Holly is associated with all that is bright and cheerful, the Yew is symbolic of sorrow, sadness, and death. Although branches of the Yew are used at Christmas-time in conjunction with Holly, Christmas does not appear to have been the time when our predecessors used it most largely ; neither does it, from its symbolic significance, appeal to one as a suitable subject to use for decorative purposes at a time when all should be bright and cheerful. Our forefathers used it extensively in conjunction with the male catkins of Salix Caprea, or Goat Willow, for church decoration in connection with the observance of Palm Sunday, and through this it came to be known as Palm. For this reason, some old writers tell us, the custom originated of planting Yews in churchyards where they did not already exist, and we learn that old Yewtrees in some country churchyards are still referred to as Palm trees. Although from the biblical account of the origin of Palm Sunday and the use of Palm leaves, we should not be inclined to associate a plant with it bearing such a lugubrious reputation as the Yew, our ancestors may, however, have brought it into use to pressage the event, the anniversary of which occurs a few days later, Good Friday.

With reference to the use of the Yew with the observance of Palm Sunday, I have come across the following note, which is an extract from *Caxton's Directions for Keeping Feasts all the Year.* In the lecture for Palm Sunday he says: "Wherefore Holy Church this day makyth solemn procefsyon, in mind of the procefsyon Cryst made this day. But for encheson that we have Olyœ that bereth grene leef, algate therefore we take Ewe instede of Palm and Olyœ, and beren in procefsyon, and so is this day called Palm Sunday."

T. baccata

Milton in the following lines appears to be describing the " Yew," though he speaks of it as Palm—

> " Cedar and Pine and Fir and branching Palm,
> A Sylvan scene! and as the ranks ascend,
> Shade above shade, a woody theatre
> Of stateliest view.
>
>   .   .   .   .   .
>
> There will I build him
> A monument, and plant it round with shade
> Of Laurel evergreen and branching Palm.
>
>   .   .   .   .
>
> He many a walk traversed
> Of stateliest covert, Cedar, Pine, or Palm."

Previous to the Christian era historians tell us that the Yew was looked on as a sacred tree, and that the vicinity of a Yew, or a group of Yews, was often a place of heathen worship. The majority of the oldest Yews in Britain are to be found in churchyards, and the generally accepted opinion prevails that these Yews were not planted as adjuncts to the churchyard, but that the churches were built near the Yews, which were already of mature years. The probability is that these old Yews were looked on as sacred trees in druidical times, and missionaries would so far respect the feelings of their converts as to erect their religious houses on, or as near as possible to, sites that had long been held sacred. In some old books the statement is made, that " when Augustine was sent

Holly, Yew and Box

by Gregory the Great to preach Christianity in
Britain, he was particularly enjoined not to
destroy the heathen temples, but only to remove
the images, to wash the walls with holy water,
to erect altars, etc., and so convert them into
Christian Churches." Some old Yews are surrounded with a circle of stones, and Loudon,
in drawing attention to this, says, that "Dr
Stukeley believes that round churches are the
most ancient in England, and that, as a circle
was a sacred symbol among the eastern nations
of antiquity, it would be interesting to know
whether the raised platform within a circle of
stones, which is sometimes found round our old
Yews, as in Darley Dale and Llanfoist churchyards, be not a remnant of this superstition."
Many of the first Christian churches are stated
to have been built and intertwined with green
boughs on the sites of druidical graves. When
Fountains Abbey in Yorkshire was founded for
the Cistercian Monks, by Archbishop Thurstan
of York, in 1132, the first Monks who went to
take possession of the land found no house, and
until the Abbey was erected they are stated to
have lived and worshipped beneath the shelter
of large Yew trees, those trees being the famous
Fountains Abbey Yews of the present day.

The fact of the Yew being found so often in
churchyards has given rise to many curious
superstitions, whilst its sombre and melancholy

appearance has not tended to improve matters. As specimens of these, the following are typical. R. Turner remarks that " if the Yew be set in a place subject to poysonous vapours, the very branches will draw and imbibe them, hence it is conceived that the judicious in former times planted it in churchyards on the west side, because those places, being fuller of putrefaction and gross oleaginous vapours exhaled out of the graves by the setting sun, and sometimes drawn by those meteors called *ignes fatui*, divers have been frightened, supposing some dead bodies to walk, etc." The questionable honour of being the most ill-omened tree in Britain must be ascribed to the Yew, if we are to judge by the old superstition, which credits it with liking better to lead a solitary life amidst the dead and sending down its roots to prey on and invigorate itself on dead bodies, rather than be sociable with its neighbours and obtain its nutriment in the manner befitting well principled trees. This superstition doubtless gave *Lord Tennyson* the idea for the following lines which occur in *In Memoriam* :—

> " Old Yew, which graspest at the stones
>   That name the underlying dead,
>   Thy fibres net the dreamless head,
>   Thy roots are wrapt about the bones."

Blair, in *The Grave*, also refers to the unsocial

Holly, Yew and Box

character of the Yew and its penchant for gloomy surroundings, for he says :—

> "Well do I know thee by thy trusty Yew,
> Cheerless, unsocial plant, that loves to dwell,
> Midst skulls and coffins, epitaphs and worms;
> Where light-heeled ghosts, and visionary shades,
> Beneath the wan cold moon (as fame reports),
> Embody'd thick perform their mystic rounds
> No other merriment, dull tree is thine."

Branches of Yew have long been used as a symbol of mourning, and in *Plant Lore* the following passage occurs in relation to it : " The Egyptians regarded it as a symbol of mourning, and the idea descended to the Greeks and Romans, who employed the wood for use in funeral pyres. The Britons probably learned from the Romans to attach a funereal signification to the Yew, and inasmuch as it had been employed in ancient funeral rites, they regarded the tree with reverence and probably looked upon it as sacred on account of age and perpetual verdure, for it was, like the Cypress, considered as a symbol of the resurrection and immortality."

Pieces of Yew are frequently used in floral tributes to the dead, and possibly this is the reason why Dryden refers to it as "The Mourner Yew" in the line—

> "The mourner Yew and builder Oak were there."

With reference to this subject *Virgil* is credited

164

with the following lines. In describing the self-
sacrifice by fire of Dido he speaks thus of the
necessary preparations :—

> " The fatal pile they rear
> Within the secret court, exposed in air.
> The cloven Holms and Pines are heaped on high,
> And garlands in the hollow spaces lie.
> Sad Cypress, Vervain, Yew, compose the wreath
> And every baleful flower denoting death. "

The death of unfortunate lovers, we are told,
was at one time made the custom for covering
biers with Yew, Willow, and Rosemary, and this
may have been the reason for *Francis Beaumont*
and *John Fletcher*, in *The Maid's Tragedy*, in-
serting the following lines :—

> " Lay a garland on my hearse
> Of the dismal Yew ;
> Maidens, Willow branches bear.
> Say that I died true."

Shakespeare alludes to the use of Yew in connection with the dead in the following lines :—

> " My shroud of white, struck all with Yew,
> Oh ! prepare it."
> —*Twelfth Night*, Act ii. Sc. 4.

In *Romeo and Juliet*, act. v. sc. 3, the Yew
is connected with churchyard associations, as
follows :—

> " Under yon Yew-tree lay thee all along,
> Holding thine ear close to the hollow ground ;
> So shall my foot upon the churchyard tread
> (Being loose, infirm, with digging up of graves)
> But thou shalt hear it."

Holly, Yew and Box

The idea that some old writers held that the Yew was planted in churchyards and used in relation to funerals on account of the mystic meaning, that its longevity was symbolic of immortality, and its evergreen character a sign of resurrection is certainly the prettiest one attached to the tree that can be included in our list.

Wordsworth probably had the idea of this allusion to immortality in mind when, in his poem on the Yew-tree, he wrote :—

> " Of vast circumference and gloom profound
> This solitary Tree ! a living thing
> Produced too slowly ever to decay ;
> Of form and aspect too magnificent
> To be destroyed."

In *Plant Lore* the following lines are quoted in reference to the ending of the troubles and trials of an arduous life after persons have been laid to rest in the churchyard :—

> " Now more I love thee melancholy Yew
> Whose still green leaves in silence wave
> Above the peasant's rude unhonoured grave,
> Which oft thou moistenest with the morning dew.
> To thee the sad, to thee the weary fly ;
> They rest in peace beneath thy sacred gloom.
> Thou sole companion of the lonely tomb ;
> No leaves but thine in pity o'er them sigh ;
> Lo ! now to fancy's gaze thou seem'st to spread
> Thy shadowy boughs to shroud me with the dead."

Apart from its reference to the dead, many writers have referred to the Yew as a gloomy or

T. baccata

sombre tree, whilst a few have been more gener-
ous and alluded to its imposing aspect.

Dyer says :—

"Behold the trees unnumber'd rise,
Beautiful in various dyes ;
The gloomy Pine, the Poplar blue,
The yellow Beech, the sombre Yew.
The slender Fir that taper grows,
The sturdy Oak with broad-spread boughs."

Prior refers to the distinguished appearance
and evergreen character of the leaves as
follows :—

"Why the changing Oak should shed,
The yearly honour of his stately head ;
Whilst the distinguished Yew is ever seen,
Unchanged his branch and permanent his green."

In *Theodric, Campbell* says :—

"There no Yew nor Cypress spread their glooms,
But Roses blossom'd by each rustic tomb."

Soliloquising on the loneliness of an isolated
Yew, Wordsworth wrote as follows ; the lines
being recorded as being left upon a seat beneath
the tree :—

"This lonely Yew-tree stands
Far from all human dwelling."

Shakespeare alludes to the dismal nature of
the Yew in the following words :—

"But straight they told me they would bind me here
Unto the body of a dismal Yew."

Titus Andronicus, Act ii. Sc. 3.

167

Holly, Yew and Box

The poisonous nature of the foliage has probably had something to do with the undesirable associations attributed to the tree, especially as these poisonous qualities were highly magnified by our forefathers of several centuries ago. Some old classical writers stated that it was certain death for anyone to lie down to sleep beneath a Yew. The following extract is from *Loudon's Arboretum et Fruticetum* : "Plutarch says that the Yew is venomous when it is in flower, because the tree is then full of sap ; and that its shade is fatal to all who sleep under it. Pliny adds to the above that the berries of the Yew are of a mortal poison, particularly in Spain ; and that persons have died, who have drunk wine out of casks made of the wood."

Gerard tells us "that *Nicander* in his book of counter poisons doth reckon the Yew-tree among the venomous plants, setting down also a remedy, and that in these words as Gorræus hath related them " :—

> "Shun the poys'nous Yew, the which on Oeata grows,
> Like to the Firre, it causes bitter death,
> Unlesse besides they use pure wine that flowes
> From empty'd cups, thou drinke, when as thy breath
> Begins to fade, and passage of thy life
> Grows straight ! "

After these ghoulish, dismal, and depressing associations, the more practical if sordid reason of the difference in money value between church-

T. baccata

yard and wood-grown Yews comes as a relief. It is rather amusing to find from *Martyn's edition of Miller* a table taken from the ancient laws of Wales, in which it states that a consecrated Yew was worth a pound, whilst a wood or lay grown specimen was worth but fifteen pence. The wonder is that the dignitaries of the Church did not think it worth while to consecrate a well-stocked forest or two.

One would naturally expect that *Sir Walter Scott*, if he wrote anything about the Yew at all, would put it in a pleasing manner.

In *The Lord of the Isles, canto v. st. xix.,* the following lines occur :—

> " And all around was verdure meet
> For pressure of the fairie's feet,
> The glossy Holly loved the park,
> The Yew-tree lent its shadow dark,
> And many an old Oak, worn and bare,
> With all its shiver'd boughs was there."

A curious, if rather horrible legend centres round a clergyman, a pretty maid, a Yew-tree, and the town of Halifax in Yorkshire. The story goes that, "a certain amorous clergyman fell in love with a pretty maid who refused his addresses. Maddened by her refusal, he cut off her head, which being hung upon a Yew-tree till it was quite decayed, the tree was reputed as sacred, not only whilst the virgin's head hung on it, but as long as the tree itself lasted ; to which

169

Holly, Yew and Box

the people went in pilgrimage, plucking and bearing away branches of it as a holy relique, whilst there remained any of the trunk; persuading themselves that those small veins and filaments resembling hairs were the hairs of the virgin. But what is stranger, the resort to this place, then called Houton, a despicable village, occasioned the building of the now famous town of Halifax in Yorkshire, the name of which imports "holy hair."

A legend respecting the sanctity of a certain tree in France is worth relating. It reads that, " In the cloister of Vreton, in Brittany, there grew a Yew tree which was said to have sprung from the staff of St Martin. Beneath it the Breton princes were accustomed to offer up a prayer before entering the church. This tree was regarded with the highest reverence; no one ever plucked a leaf from its sombre boughs, and even the birds refrained from pecking the scarlet berries. A band of pirates, however, happening to visit the locality, two of them spied the tree, and forthwith climbed into its venerable branches and proceeded to cut bow staves for themselves; their audacity speedily brought its own punishment, for they both fell and were killed on the spot." See *Plant Lore*.

Superstitious persons who place reliance on dreams may be interested to know that to dream

T. baccata

of a Yew-tree does not signify that something dreadful is about to happen, although the tree is so often associated with unpleasant thoughts, for dream experts explain, we learn from *Plant Lore*, that to dream of a Yew-tree forecasts the death of an aged person, through which the dreamer will derive substantial benefit.

XIX

T. BACCATA—*Continued*

Uses

AT the present time the uses of the Yews may be said to be purely decorative, for, although the timber is used to some extent, trees are not largely planted for economic purposes. As decorative plants the Yews are almost as useful as the Hollies, and they may be used for very similar purposes. Notwithstanding the many lugubrious remarks made about the " Common Yew " on account of its dark and sombre appearance, it has much to commend it for landscape work, and either groups or single trees are very effective in winter, when deciduous trees are bare, whilst in summer the dark foliage contrasts well with the many shades of green found on other trees. Apart from the type there is a large number of garden varieties, which includes many first-rate decorative subjects. These differ from the type either in colour or habit, and can be used for many purposes about the garden. As isolated specimens they are effective, whilst they group excellently,

and some are useful for avenues. As a hedge
plant the Yew is almost as popular as the Holly,
and many exceptionally fine hedges are to be
found composed entirely of "Common Yew."
For naturally damp and heavy ground it is more
appropriate than Holly, whilst it has an advantage over that plant on account of its fine growth
and small leaves. When at its best it forms a
very dense, and practically an impenetrable
hedge, and rarely requires more than an annual
clipping to keep it in good order. Owing to the
extreme age the Yew attains, when once a
hedge is thoroughly established there is little
fear of its having to be replaced.

The bark of the Yew is sometimes used for
tea in India, according to specimens and descriptions exhibited in the Kew Museums. This is
suggestive of the poisonous qualities found in
the leaves being absent from the bark after it
has been dried, or found only in such quantities
as to cause no serious harm. Medicinally, the
tree seems to have been of no value, though
Canon Ellacombe, in *Plant Lore of Shakespeare*,
records an instance of the fruit being used in
conjunction with various other things in the
preparation of a certain Anglo-Saxon medicine.
The recipe for this medicine is well worth
recording, and is as follows, with Canon Ellacombe's introduction: "There is no doubt that
the Yew berries are almost if not quite harm-

less, and I find them forming an element in an Anglo-Saxon recipe, which may be worth quoting as an example of the medicines to which our forefathers submitted. It is given in a leech-book of the tenth century or earlier, and is thus translated by Cockayne: 'If a man is in the water elf disease, then are the nails of his hands livid, and the eyes tearful, and he will look downwards. Give him this for a leechdom. Everthroat, Cassuck, the netherward part of Fane, a Yew berry, Lupin, Helenium, a head of Marsh Mallow, Fen, Mint, Dill, Lily, Attorlothe, Pulegium, Marrubium, Dock, Elder, Felterræ, Wormwood, Strawberry leaves, Consolida ; pour them over with ale, add holy water, and sing this charm over them thrice.'" The charm is not given by Canon Ellacombe, but may be seen in *Cockayne's* work, *vol. ii.*; *Leech Book, iii. p.* 351 ; *Leechdom, lxiii.* When we find that a sick man 1000 years ago was given medicine such as the above-mentioned compost, and was expected to get well after taking it, we are inclined to ponder over the constitution of such a man, compared with men's constitutions of to-day, and also as to whether the leech was not really actuated with the idea that by giving the man a little of each of his herbs he might find one among them that would answer his purpose, or failing that, the ale, holy water, charm, or what not, might have the desired effect.

T. baccata

Evelyn records an instance of a family of three children being killed by being given a liquid prepared from Yew leaves for some childish complaint. These children were unwell, and neighbours recommended a decoction of Yew leaves as a remedy. The first mixture that was given was prepared from dried leaves, and this appears to have done the children no harm ; two nights later a second mixture was made from fresh leaves ; an hour or two later the children were attacked by sickness, and within a few hours all died.

The wood of the Yew is very strong, hard, tough, and durable. It was at one period in demand for making cogs for mills, axletrees for carts, posts, etc., whilst it was of considerable repute for inlaying work. It is one of the most durable woods known, and posts placed in wet ground last longer than Oak. The use, however, for which the wood of the Yew attained its greatest popularity was for the making of bows for archery purposes. Used for this purpose it has had a great deal to do with European history, as the bow was one of the principal weapons in ancient warfare. At the battle of Hastings, William The Conqueror's Archers had a great deal to do with the defeat of the Saxons, whilst we read that King Harold lost his life through being shot in the eye with an arrow. A few years later William II. was killed

Holly, Yew and Box

in the New Forest by an arrow, whilst during
the next two or three centuries archers took a
foremost part in all battles.   At the battle of
Cressy, fought on August 25th, 1346, we read
that "the French troops included a number of
Genœse archers, but that the nobility of France
held archers in contempt.   In the early part of
the battle a shower of rain came on which
thoroughly wet the archers' bowstrings ; on being
ordered to discharge their arrows they were
unable to do so on account of wet strings, this
so enraged Philip VI. that he ordered his
mounted troops to ride them down.   The English archers, meanwhile, had kept their bows in
cases during the shower, and so kept them dry,
and as they had been long accustomed to shoot
strongly at a mark, they made short work of the
French horsemen."   Ten years later, at Poitiers,
the Black Prince ambushed King John of
France, enticing his soldiers down a narrow
lane, to be shot down by English archers from
behind the hedges on either hand.   Other battles
in which archers with their long bows figured
conspicuously were Agincourt, The War of the
Roses, Falkirk, and Flodden Field.

During the sixteenth century there seems to
have been an idea that the use of the bow was
inclined to be neglected, for we find that Henry
the Eighth took steps to encourage archery
throughout the country.   During this reign a

T. baccata

scholar, *Roger Ascham*, wrote a very amusing book entitled, *Toxophilus, The Schoole of Shooting*, and this book he claims to have been the first ever written on the subject. From the manner in which the book is written we should imagine Mr Ascham to have been a very precise and crotchety old gentleman. Although the book affords the reader of the present day much amusement, it was not intended by the author to be anything but really serious business. His decision to write the book was made during the war with France which took place during the reign of Henry VIII., and in the introductory chapter he gives his reasons for attempting the work. The following, in his own quaint language, is a portion of the introduction :—

" To all Gentle men and Yoemen of Englande."

. . . . .

" By this matter I meane the fhotying in the long bowe, for Englifh men ; which thyng with all my hert I do wyth, and I were of authorite, I wolde compel all the gentle men and yoemen of Englande, not to chaunge it with any other thyng to be; but that ftyll, accordyng to theoulde wont of Englande youth fhoulde vfe it for the mooft honeft paftyme in peace, that men myght handle it as a mooft fure weapon in warre."

In describing the battles of Cressy, Poitiers,

177

and Agincourt he says: "Kynge Edward the Third at the battle of Creſſie ageinſt Philip ye Frenche Kynge, as Gaguinus the French Hiſtoriographer plainlye doeth tell, ſlewe that daye all the nobilite of Fraunce onlye wyth hys archers."

"Such lyke battel alſo fought ye noble Black Prince Edwarde befide Pœters, where John ye French Kynge with his ſonne and in a manner al ye peers of Fraunce were taken befid xxx thouſand which that daye were ſlayne, and verie few Englyſhe men by reaſon of theyr bowes."

"Kynge Henrie the Fifth a prince pereles and moſt vyctorioufe conqueroure of all that ever dyed yet in this parte of the wourlde, at the battel of Agincourt with vii thousand fyghtynge men and yet many of them fycke beynge ſuch Archers as the Cronycle ſayeth that moſte parte of them drewe a yarde, ſlew all the Cheualrie of Fraunce to the nomber of xl thousand and moo, and loſt not paſte xxvi Englyſhe men."

Over the horrors of the Civil War betwixt the houses of York and Lancaster he prefers to draw a veil, saying that "shafts flew from both sides, to the destruction of many a yeoman whom foreign battle could never have subdued."

One passage shows him to have been a patriot if nothing else. A continental writer, *Texter*, had made the remark that, "the Scottes which dwell beyonde Englande be verye excellent

T. baccata

fhoters and the best bowmen in warre." Ascham
became very wrathful at this, and took up the
cudgels for the English, saying that if Texter
had looked no further than Kent he would have
found better archers. The Scotts, he says, are
surely good men of war in their own way ; but
as for shooting they can neither use it with any
use or profit. He goes on to say that James the
First of Scotland, at the Parliament held at
St John's town, or Perth, commanded under pain
of a great forfit that every Scot should learn to
shoot ; yet neither the love of their country, the
fear of their enemies, punishment, or the receiving
of any profit that might come of it, could make
them to be good archers, which they may be
unapt and unfit for by God's providence and good
nature." In one place, when sounding the praises
of the bow, he says that, "although he knows
that God is the only giver of victory, and not the
weapons, for all strength and victory come from
heaven ; yet surely strong weapons be the instruments wherewith God doth overcome the part
which he will have overthrown, for *God is well
pleased with wise and wittie feats of war.*"

In his description of the making of bows he
says : "Every bow is made either of a bough, of
a plant, or of the bole. The bough commonly is
very knotty and full of pins, weak, of small pith,
and fane will follow the string, and seldom weareth
to any fair colour, yet for children and young

M 179

beginners it may serve well enough. The plant proveth many times well if it be a good and clean growth, and for the pith, if it is quick enough cast, it will ply and bow before it break, as all young things do. The bole of the tree is cleanest, without knots or pins, having a safe and hard wood by reason of its full growth and might of cast, and is best for a bow if the staves be even cloven and be afterwards wrought, not over athwart the wood, but as the grain and strength-growing of the wood leadeth a man, or else by all reason it must fane break, and that in many shivers."

He also tells how to select a bow, and the following is the advice he gives : " If you come into a shoppe and fynde a bowe that is small, longe, heavye, stronge, lyinge streighte, not wyndynge, nor marred with knotts, gaule, wynd-shake, wem, freat, or pinch, bye that bowe on my warrant."

He moralises here and there, and uses proverbs to point his morals. One is, "A good bow twice paid for is better than an ill bow once broken." In referring to archery in Scotland, he says that the Scots had a proverb to the effect that "every English bowman carried 24 Scotts under his girdle"—meaning that every English arrow would account for a Scot.

The use made of the wood for bows has caused the Yew to be spoken of as the Shooter Eugh,

T. baccata

and Fairfax quotes this name in the following lines:—

> " The shooter *Eugh*, the broad leaved Sycamore,
> The barren Plantane and the Walnut round;
> The Myrtle, that her foul sin doth still deplore;
> Alder, the owner of all waterish ground."

Spenser, in *The Færie Queen, Bk. I., Canto* 1, *St.* 8, refers to the qualities of various trees, and to the use of the Yew for the bow as follows :—

> " And foorth they passe with pleasure forward led,
> Joying to hear the birdes sweete harmony,
> Which, therein shrouded from the tempest dread,
> Seemed in their song to scorn the cruel sky.
> Much can they praise the trees so straight and hy.
> The sayling Pine; the Cedar proud and tall;
> The Vine-propp Elme; the Poplar, never dry;
> The builder Oake, sole king of forrests all;
> The Aspine good for staves; the Cypresse funeral.
> The Laurel, meed of mightie conquerours;
> The *Eugh*, obedient to the bender's will;
> The Birch for shafts; the Sallow for the mill;
> The Mirrhe sweete, bleeding in the bitter wound;
> The warlike Beech; the Ash for nothing ill;
> The fruitful Olive; and the Platane round;
> The carver Holme; the Maple, seldom inward sound."

One of the prettiest legends attached to the Yew centres round the use of the bow, and it is at the same time illustrative of patriotism, courage, and nerve under most trying circumstances. This is the Swiss story of William Tell. The legend goes, that the Swiss were oppressed by their rulers, the Austrians, and on one occasion in 1307, when the Austrian ruler wished to show how he was all-powerful over his subjects, he placed his hat upon a staff in Altorf market-place, and ordered all the Swiss to bow down to it. When it came to Tell's turn he refused to obey such a ridiculous order, and as a result was condemned to death. He had, however, attained great renown as a marksman, and the Austrian Duke, wishing for an exhibition of his skill, ordered him to divide an apple with an arrow, shot from a considerable distance, the apple being placed on the head of Tell's son. The feat was performed without accident, but it marked a new era in the history of Switzerland, for it was the signal for a general uprising by means of which the Swiss were enabled to throw off the foreign yoke. Through this association between William Tell and the Yew-tree it is still spoken of in Switzerland as " William's Tree."

Although the use of the bow appears to have been most popular in England from the twelfth to the fifteenth century, it was in use long before the Battle of Hastings, whilst as a pastime archery is still encouraged. Both ancient and modern archery is dealt with in *C. J. Longman* and *Col. H. Walrond's* book on *Archery*, a book which contains a vast amount of information on the subject. A bow is described as being dug up in Cambridge in 1855 from deep down in a bed of peat. It was impossible to discover its date, but the authors consider that it probably dated back to prehistoric times. It consisted of a single stave of Yew 4 ft. $11\frac{1}{2}$ inches long, perfect, except for about one inch being broken off one end. Archery as a pastime was indulged in at one period almost to the exclusion of other sports, and all men and youths were expected to practise assiduously every Sunday and on all holidays, whilst in Scotland Robert the Bruce ordered every person worth a cow to have a spear, or a good bow and sheath of 24 arrows, and they were expected to practise on every possible occasion. Men above twenty-four years of age were not expected at one period to shoot at a mark at a less distance than 220 yards. Loudon records that in the reign of Edward VI. every Englishman dwelling in Ireland was expressly ordered to have an English bow of his own height, made of Yew, Wych, Hazel, Ash, Awburne or Laburnum. Referring to the various kinds of wood used for bows, Roger Ascham says :—" As for Brasell, Elme, Wych, and Ashe, experience doth prove them to be mean for bowes ; and so to conclude Ewe of all other things is that whereof perfite shootinge would have a bowe made." At the present time several rather strong archery clubs exist, but archery cannot claim to be a national pastime, for although youths, after a first perusal of Robin Hood, are fired with enthusiasm to emulate the doughty

Holly, Yew and Box

deeds of Robin Hood, Little John, and other celebrities, their ardour soon cools in face of the more exciting attractions of football and cricket.

In *Pennant's London, ed. III., p.* 39, it is stated that "in 1397, Richard II., holding a parliament in a temporary building, on account of the wretched state of Westminster Hall, surrounded his hut with 4000 Cheshire archers armed with tough Yew bows, to insure freedom of debate." One is sometimes inclined to think that such an arrangement might have a beneficial effect upon debates in present-day politics.

XX

T. BACCATA—*Continued*

Large Trees

NUMEROUS records have been made of famous old trees. Loudon calls attention to the principal ones in his *Arboretum et Fruticetum Britannicum*; in 1897 a book by the late *John Lowe, M.D.*, on the *Yew-trees of Great Britain and Ireland* was published, whilst, in *The Trees of Great Britain and Ireland*, by *Mr Elwes* and *Dr A. Henry*, numerous other instances of famous trees are recorded. Mr Elwes describes the Yews in the Close Walk at Midhurst as probably the most remarkable Yew-grove in Britain or elsewhere, and gives a reference of Queen Elizabeth having been entertained to a banquet beneath these Yews. The trees are said to be from 75 to 80 feet high. At Downton, Wilts, there is stated to be a wood of large Yews 80 acres in extent belonging to the Earl of Radnor, called "The Great Yews."

The large Yew-tree in the churchyard at Darley Dale is one of our most famous trees.

Holly, Yew and Box

It is stated to be at the present time about 50 feet in height with a girth of 32 feet 3 inches at four feet from the ground. An illustration of it may be seen in the Wood Museum at Kew, with a foot-note saying that the tree is estimated as being about 2000 years old.

Mention has previously been made of the "Fountains Abbey Yews," which are of great size. A very large tree, estimated to be upwards of 1000 years of age, stands in Buckland church-yard, near Dover. The trunk of this girths 22 feet, or did according to a description in the *Gardener's Chronicle* in 1880. In March of that year, although the tree was so old, it was success-fully transplanted. The ball of soil taken with the tree was 16 feet 5 inches by 11 feet 8 inches by 3 feet 6½ inches deep, the entire mass weigh-ing about 56 tons. In *Lauder's Gilpin*, reference is made to a large Yew standing on the left bank of Lymington river looking towards the sea, which is described as a very fine specimen. The Yew-tree Island in Loch Lomond is also mentioned, the author stating it furnished 300 Yews at one cutting, and that a number of fine specimens were still left. A large Yew is also described as growing far from cultivation and human dwellings, in the midst of the wild country between Loch Ness and the sources of the river Findhorn. The famous "Fortingal Yew" in Perthshire also comes in for notice, and of this

T. baccata

tree a very good illustration is presented in *Strutt's Sylva Britannica.* When in full vigour the trunk of this was variously stated to be from 50 to 56½ feet in circumference, and that when it became hollow it divided into two parts, and funeral processions were in the habit of passing through it. Strutt's illustration shows such a procession. Strutt also gives a picture of the "Fountains Abbey Yews," and another of the "Ankerwyke Yew" which stands in the grounds attached to Ankerwyke House at Staines. This latter tree is stated to overlook the famous island in the Thames where Magna Charta was signed, and it was probably a mature tree at that time. It is also of historic interest as figuring as a trysting place between Henry VIII. and Anne Boleyn, and the following poem describing the two events which the tree witnessed is given by Strutt :—

> "What scenes have pass'd since first this ancient Yew
> In all the strength of youthful beauty grew!
> Here patriot Britons might have musing stood,
> And plann'd the Charta for their Country's good;
> And here, perhaps, from Runnymede retired,
> The haughty John with secret vengeance fired,
> Might curse the day which saw his weakness yield
> Extorted rights in yonder tented field.
> Here too the tyrant Henry felt love's flame
> And, sighing, breathed his Anna Boleyn's name.
> Beneath the shelter of this Yew-tree's shade
> The royal lover woo'd the ill-starr'd maid,
> And yet that neck round which he fondly hung,

187

Holly, Yew and Box

To hear the thrilling accents of her tongue ;
That lovely breast, on which his head reclined,
Form'd to have humanised his savage mind ;
Were doomed to bleed beneath the tyrant's heel,
Whose selfish heart could dote but could not feel ! "

In the churchyard at Harlington, a village about four miles out from Hounslow on the Bath road, a fine old Yew may be seen (see illustration). At the present time it is about 50 or 55 feet high, with a girth at 4½ feet above the ground of 21 feet 3 inches, and a diameter across the lower branches of about 60 feet. Loudon refers to this tree, and says that it was formerly fantastically clipped. He gives a copy of an illustration of it as it appeared in 1729. This shows a very curious looking tree, rising by means of two or three wide, table-like storeys to a globe, surmounted by a weather-cock, the interspaces being thick, round, green columns. The original illustration was accompanied by a poem composed by the parish clerk, whose name was John Saxey. In reference to the lower part he says that it was—

" So thick, so fine, so full, so wide,
A troup of guards might under it ride."

The weather - cock came in for notice as follows :—

" A weather-cock, who gaped to crow it,
This world is mine and all below it."

I saw this tree on February 2nd of the present

"THE HARLINGTON YEW," IN HARLINGTON CHURCHYARD,
MIDDLESEX

year, and it appears to be in the best of health
and shows no sign of its former clipping. The
trunk is remarkable for its burrs and swollen
portions, which cause the girth to differ considerably in the space of a few inches, a foot higher
than the place where my measurement was taken
will probably girth 2 feet more, whilst at 8 feet,
where it divides into two trunks, it is even more.
The churchyard contains a second tree of good
size. It is about 40 feet high and the trunk is
13 feet in diameter at 4 feet above the ground, a
place where it is rather curiously swollen. Other
places where large trees are recorded are in
Mamhilad churchyard, a few miles north of
Pontypool; at Llanthewy Vach near Cærleon;
in Gresford churchyard, Derbyshire; in Iffley
churchyard, Oxfordshire; Tirbury churchyard,
Dorsetshire; Tytherley churchyard, Wiltshire;
near this latter an avenue of Yews 414 yards
long, consisting of 162 trees, is also recorded;
at Crom Castle, the seat of Lord Erne, there is
a tree which is said to cover $\frac{1}{8}$ of an acre of
ground, this was planted 1100 years ago. Several
old trees are to be seen at "The Hendre," the
Monmouthshire seat of Lord Llangattock; one
of these I measured in June 1907 and found it
to be 18½ feet in girth at 3 feet above the ground.
In addition to these many other large examples
have been recorded, but space will not allow of
their inclusion.

Holly, Yew and Box

Topiary Work

For topiary work the Yew has long been famous, and although it is not the oldest subject that has been used for the purpose it has perhaps been used more than any other. Its small foliage and naturally close habit has been greatly in its favour for this particular kind of work, whilst the manner in which it will stand cropping year after year stamped it at once as a likely subject. Evelyn claims to have been the first person to discover its merits for this work, and in Evelyn's time topiary work was popular, comparatively small specimens being worth £5 each. Although this kind of work does not find much favour among horticulturists nowadays, there are still gardens where a speciality is made of it, and in many gardens one or more examples of the work may be found. Two gardens noted for topiary work are Leven's Hall, Westmorland, and Elvaston Castle near Derby. Two curiously clipped trees, about 20 feet in height, may be seen in the churchyard at Bedfont in Middlesex, about 2½ miles on the Staines side of Hounslow. They stand close to the church door and just behind them the wooden steeple rises, the whole having a quaint appearance. The formal appearance of these clipped trees is intensified by a fine naturally grown tree of the same sort growing on one side and a Weeping Willow on

T. baccata

the other. For further particulars about topiary work, see *The Book of Topiary Work. John Lane.*

Cultivation

The Yew may be grown in almost any kind of garden soil, but thrives best in that of a moist and loamy nature. On chalky soil it succeeds well, whilst it is also met with in very sandy soil and growing in crevices of rocks. When transplanted with a good ball of soil, the work may be done at any period between early September and the latter end of May, but if transplanted without soil it should be done very early in the autumn or late in spring. Many thousands of plants are raised from seeds annually, whilst the varieties are increased by means of cuttings or by grafting on stocks of the type. Cuttings of small shoots, taken during July and August, and inserted in sandy soil under a hand-light or placed in pots in a close case root readily. Growth for the first year or two is slow, but after that period it becomes more rapid. Any necessary pruning is best done during early summer, as this will allow the season's growth to cover up the old cuts. Hedges and specimen plants that appear to be weakening can be improved by top-dressing with well-rotted manure and leaves. The Hon. Vicary Gibbs states that Yews may be got to grow more rapidly by giving them

Holly, Yew and Box

an occasional dressing of nitrate of soda. For planting in shady places the Yew has much to commend it, for it thrives under the shade of trees where most other plants refuse to grow. Groups composed of the golden foliaged varieties form a very striking feature in the landscape, whilst the fastigiate habited sorts are useful for forming avenues where the surroundings are of a more or less formal character. As isolated specimens for lawns and other open spaces, many of the varieties have much to recommend them, especially if they are allowed to grow naturally instead of being clipped into globes or pyramids as is too often the case.

XXI

T. BACCATA—*continued*

Varieties

T. B. adpressa, *Carriere* = adpressa, *Gordon*; brevifolia, *Hort*; and sinensis tardiva, *Knight.*—This is a very distinct variety, quite different in appearance from any other Yew, and by some people thought deserving of specific rank. It is recognised by its rounded, bush-like habit, which never affects a central leader, and small, blunt, evenly arranged leaves. It grows into a large wide-spreading bush of uniform shape, and, with little or no attention to pruning, forms a handsome specimen.

T. b. adpressa aurea resembles the former in every respect, except that the leaves are golden variegated. The late Messrs Standish, Nurserymen, of Ascot, are credited with its introduction.

T. b. adpressa stricta.—This has been given numerous names, such as adpressa erecta, adpressa fastigiata and verticillata. Its chief peculiarity is its stiff upright habit and less dense leafage than the type.

Holly, Yew and Box

T. b. adpressa variegata differs from the others by having some of the shoots variegated with white. It is, however, less handsome than the golden variety.

T. b. argentea.—A form with silver variegated leaves. The variegation consists of silver marginal stripes on the under surface of the young leaves and a greyish upper surface; much of the colour is lost before winter. It is less ornamental than the golden-leaved varieties.

T. b. albo-variegata. — This variety is recognised by means of some of the leaves being variegated with white. The variegation is not, however, evenly distributed, being confined to portions of branches here and there. As an ornamental garden plant it has few pretensions, and is only worthy of notice in those gardens where full collections of varieties are aimed at.

T. b. aurea.—A variety of compact habit, with pretty golden variegated leaves. As in most of the golden-leaved Yews, the colour is most brilliant on the under surface, that on the upper side being often but narrow marginal lines, whilst the under side is golden throughout. As the leaves have a peculiar method of showing their under-surfaces, the full value of the colouring is gained. The gold colour is retained only during the first year, changing to green afterwards. A great deal of latitude has to be given this variety, for forms are to be found which

1. I. BACCATA GRACILIS PENDULA,   2. I. CUSPIDATA,   GROUP OF YEWS

3. I. B. ELEGANTISSIMA

T. baccata

exhibit a wide range of habit and colouring, probably due to being raised from seeds.

T. b. aurea variegata.—This differs from the last-named, principally in habit, the general effect being looser.

T. b. Barroni.—One of the most showy of the golden-leaved varieties, the habit being dense and the colour very rich. It stands out distinct from other Yews by reason of the rich coppery colour of the foliage ; the young shoots are also of a deeper orange than those of other varieties. The upper surface of the leaves is more richly coloured than most other varieties.

T. b. brevifolia—This must not be confused with the species from Western North America, known as T. brevifolia, nor with the variety adpressa, which numbers among its synonyms the name of brevifolia. The true variety brevifolia forms a medium-sized bush with small, densely arranged leaves, which rarely exceed half an inch in length, and during winter assume a bronzy hue.

T. b. Dovastoni, *Carr.* = Dovastoni, *Hort* ; pendula, *Hort*; and umbraculifera, *Hort.*—Of the many varieties, this is certainly one of the most handsome. It is easily recognised from other sorts by reason of the pendulous or weeping character of the branchlets. Standing on a lawn away from other plants it is a most imposing object, and always attracts attention. The

Holly, Yew and Box

original plant grew in the garden of J. F. M. Dovaston, Esq., of Westfelton, near Shrewsbury, and for this reason was given the common names of "Dovaston Yew" and "Westfelton Yew." Loudon gives the history of the origin of the variety, and it is worth repeating. He says : "The Westfelton Yew stands in the grounds of J. F. M. Dovaston, Esq., of Westfelton, near Shrewsbury, and the following account has been sent to us by that gentleman : 'About 60 years ago (now nearly 130), my father, John Dovaston, a man without education, but of unwearied industry and ingenuity, had, with his own hands, sunk a well and constructed and placed a pump in it, and the soil being light and sandy it constantly fell in. He secured it with wooden boards, but, perceiving their speedy decay, he planted near the well a Yew tree, which he bought of a cobbler for sixpence, rightly judging that the fibrous and matting tendency of the Yew roots would hold up the soil. They did so, and, independently of its utility, the Yew grew into a tree of extraordinary and striking beauty, spreading horizontally all round, with a single aspiring leader to a great height, each branch in every direction dangling in tressy verdure downwards, the lowest ones to the very ground, pendulous and playful as the most graceful Birch or Willow, and visibly obedient to the feeblest breath of air. Though a male tree, it has one

T. baccata

branch self-productive, and profuse of berries, from which I have raised several plants in the hope that they may inherit some of the beauty of their parent.'" In *The Garden, Vol. ix. p.* 341, it is stated that this tree was flourishing in 1876, and that its height was 34 feet, girth of trunk 7½ feet, and circumference of head 72 feet.

T. b. Dovastoni aureo-variegata.—A form similar in habit to the last mentioned, but having leaves beautifully variegated with gold. It is one of the most conspicuous of the golden-leaved sorts.

T. b. elegantissima.—This variety originated in the Handsworth Nurseries. It is of vigorous habit and elegant appearance, forming a wide spreading bush, the main branches more or less horizontal, with the secondary branches pendulous. The young leaves and shoots are of a pale gold colour, relieved on the upper surface with streaks of green. In point of size the leaves range from ¾ of an inch to 1¼ inches long. It forms a handsome specimen.

T. b. epacridioides. — A rather small-leaved sort, the leaves rarely exceeding ½ an inch in length. It forms a medium-sized bush with upright growth, but is not stiff in appearance. During winter the leaves take on a bronzy hue.

T. b. erecta = baccata stricta and Crowderi.— A variety recognised by its close upright habit

Holly, Yew and Box

of growth and somewhat stiff outline. The leaves are deep green and of medium size, rarely exceeding ¾ of an inch in length. Although of upright habit, it forms a much more spreading plant than the "Irish Yew."

T. b. ericoides = empetrifolia, microphylla, and Mitchelli. — This forms but a low growing bush, and cannot be called ornamental. The leaves are small and of a bronzy or purplish colour in winter. It is a suitable subject for planting on rockwork.

T. b. expansa.—A very distinct, green-leaved variety of upright growth and good habit. It is readily distinguished among other varieties by its comparatively large leaves, from 1 to 1½ inches long, which show the pale green of the reverse side rather conspicuously, forming a striking contrast to the rich dark green of the upper surface. It is of rapid growth, and worthy attention for general planting.

T. b. fastigiata, *Loudon* = T. hibernica, *Hooker*; and "The Irish Yew." — This, like the variety adpressa, is quite distinct in general appearance from the type. It is of upright habit, resembling in character the "Lombardy Poplar." The leaves are very dark green, and are more scattered on the branches than are those of the type. It is useful for planting in positions where a spreading tree would be out of place, whilst it can be advantageously used for

IRISH OR FLORENCE COURT YEW.   IN THE GARDEN OF THE LATE
DUKE OF CAMBRIDGE, KEW

T. baccata

groups and avenues for various styles of gardening. Although, when mature, it forms a large specimen with a somewhat loose branch arrangement, younger plants are very dense in habit and form a compact column. Trees are easily kept in this form by going over them once a year and shortening the ends of branches that are inclined to become too heavy for their own weight and bend outwards instead of keeping erect. It was first noticed growing on the mountains of Fermanagh, near Florence Court, which accounts for the name of "The Florence Court Yew" which is sometimes applied to it. A reprint in the *Gardener's Chronicle* for 1873, p. 1336, from the *People's Journal* gives the following account of this variety : "Near by our place is a grave marked by a small and solitary Irish Yew, and nothing more. I know not who had laid under it. That dark green 'mournful Yew,' however, serves a purpose in some hearts. Here and there are to be seen similar monuments breaking the monotony of the grassy ranges. Each of them seems to have a sad story in its custody. The dark Yew has long been adapted as a favourite tree for shading the ground of our dead. The Irish Yew, or Florence Court variety of the Yew, has in a special manner become the most prominent and distinguished of the family. The history of the Irish Yew may be of interest to many. Here it

Holly, Yew and Box

is, and I quote from the MS. in possession of Lord Kinnaird : 'Above one hundred years ago, Mr Willis, farmer, of Aghenteroark, in the parish of Killesher, county of Fermanagh, found upon his farm on the mountains above Florence Court, two plants of this tree. These he dug up, and planted one in his own garden. He took the other down to his landlord at Mount Florence, where it was planted. The tree that was planted in his own garden, remained there till the year 1865, when it died. The other is still alive at Florence Court, and is the one from which the millions of plants now distributed in all parts have sprung. The first cuttings were given by my father, the Earl of Enniskillen, to Messrs Lee and Kennedy, then the largest nurserymen about London.'—Signed, Enniskellen, Rossie Priory, September 8, 1867." Some people recommend that this plant should be made a distinct species, but from most people's experience it cannot be relied on to come true from seeds. Mr Mackay, in Flora Hibernica, p. 260, says that the finest specimens of this variety grow at Comber, near Antrim, County Down, and that they are supposed to have been planted about 1780. A figure of the original Irish Yew at Florence Court is given in *Veitch's Conifer Manual, ed. i., p. 303.*

T. b. fastigiata argentea is so called by reason of the silver variegation of some of the

T. baccata

leaves. The variegation is not constant, however.

T. b. fastigiata aurea, *Standish* = hibernica aurea, and "Golden Irish Yew."—Like the majority of the golden Yews the colour of the leaves of this variety is best on the under-surface, that on the upper side being intermixed with green. It is a very conspicuous variety, and varies somewhat in colour according to the nursery from which it is procured.

T. b. fastigiata grandis.—A selected form of the "Golden Irish Yew," with the golden colouring more prominently developed on the upper surface.

T. b. fastigiata Standishii. — As in the case of the foregoing, this is a very richly coloured form of the "Golden Irish Yew."

T. b. Fisheri.—This is a green-leaved variety of spreading habit. The main branches are developed more or less horizontally, and there is no special leader. It forms a very nice bush.

T. b. Foxii. — A small-leaved variety of spreading habit, forming a low, compact bush, suitable for a position on rockwork. It grows slowly, especially in height.

T. b. fructu-luteo.—This resembles the type in every respect, save that the fleshy covering of the fruit is of a golden colour. It fruits freely and is very attractive in autumn. When growing near a red-fruited plant the contrast between

Holly, Yew and Box

the gold and red is very effective. Loudon records fine trees at Clontarf Castle, near Dublin, and speaks as follows of its origin : " It appears to have been first discovered by a Mr Whitlaw, of Dublin, about 1817, or before, growing on the lands of the Bishop of Kildare, near Glasnevin ; but it seems to have been neglected till 1833, when it was noticed in the grounds of Clontarf Castle, whence cuttings were distributed."

T. b. glauca, *Carr* = subglaucescens and nigra. —The principal peculiarity of this lies in the fact of the young leaves being of a glaucous hue. This glaucous colouring, however, is not retained throughout the year, and when it is gone there is nothing to distinguish the variety from an ordinary Yew.

T. b. gracilis pendula.—This is a vigorous habited variety with deep green foliage. The main branches are more or less horizontal, and from them the secondary branches hang gracefully to a depth of several feet. It forms a natural leader, and grows into a handsome specimen.

T. b. horizontalis.—This variety is readily recognised by reason of its branches being borne in a horizontal position and no leader being produced. It forms a wide spreading bush with several tiers of branches, and is of a very deep green colour.

T. b. horizontalis elegantissima.—A form very

similar in habit to horizontalis, but having golden, variegated leaves. It comes nearest to elegantissima, but the branches are developed more horizontally than in that variety.

T. b. imperialis.—An upright-growing plant of compact habit, but less stiff in appearance than fastigiata. The leaves are medium-sized, and dark green.

T. b. nana.—A low-growing shrub, rarely attaining a height of 3 feet, but forming a wide spreading mass. The leaves are small, and deep green. It looks well growing on the higher parts of a rockery.

T. b. neidpathensis = "Neidpath Yew."—This is a bold, vigorous-habited, green-leaved variety. The branches are erect, but there is no approach to stiffness about the plant.

T. b. pendula.—This is very similar in appearance to gracilis pendula, but the habit is somewhat looser, and the growth less robust. It, however, forms a handsome lawn specimen.

T. b. procumbens.—A prostrate-growing variety, somewhat like nana, but having rather longer leaves and stronger branches.

T. b. pyramidalis.—A green-leaved variety of rather stiff outline. The upright branches are crowded together, and rather sparingly clothed with secondary branches. It is not one of the most ornamental varieties.

T. b. pyramidalis variegata resembles pyramidalis in habit, but the leaves are variegated with gold.

T. b. recurvata, *Carr* = T. recurvata.—This is a strong-growing, green-leaved variety, remarkable for the manner in which the leaves are recurved. The branches are developed horizontally, and it forms a large, wide-spreading plant without any definite leader.

T. b. semperaurea. — A golden variegated variety of rather low growth, chiefly remarkable by the leaves retaining much of their colour during the second year, whereas in most golden-leaved varieties the colour is lost after the first year.

T. b. sinensis, *Knight.* — This is a rather small green-leaved variety, which does not differ materially from the type. The original plant was of Chinese origin.

T. b. Washingtoni = canadensis Washingtoni. —A golden-leaved sort of widely-spreading habit, with no distinct leader. The leaves are from 1 to $1\frac{1}{4}$ inches long, and the colour is most pronounced on the undersurface.

Other Species

T. brevifolia, *Nuttall* = " The Californian Yew." —Although not in general cultivation in England, this would thrive well enough in the milder counties. In California it is said to attain

T. baccata

about the same dimensions that T. baccata does in England. The leaves are smaller than those of the "Common Yew," being rarely more than two-thirds of an inch long. They are also paler in colour. It is doubtful whether the plant is a really good species, and some people consider it to be a geographical form of T. baccata. It was introduced by the Veitchian Collector, William Lobb, in 1854.

T. canadensis, *Willdenow* = "The Canadian Yew."—This is really the N. American form of the "Common Yew," and it is difficult to detect any real distinctive marks between the two. It is fairly widely distributed through Canada and the north-eastern States. Under cultivation it forms a moderate-sized bush with rather dense growth and smallish leaves. The fruits are somewhat smaller than those of T. baccata. There is a variety with golden variegated leaves.

T. cuspidata, *Siebold* and *Zuccarini* = "Japanese Yew."—This species is said to exist in a limited area, only, in Japan, that being on the low hills of the interior of the island of Yezo. It is stated to attain there a height of from 40 to 50 feet, with a trunk diameter of 24 inches. The bark is red, and the wood is said to be used for bows by the Ainos. It is also in demand for cabinet-making, and for the indoor decoration of the best houses. It is less dense in habit than our own Yew, and has thicker and more pointed

Holly, Yew and Box

leaves, which are of a yellowish-green colour. Under cultivation it differs considerably in appearance, sometimes being of pyramidal outline and again a low spreading bush. A dwarf variety has been introduced, which is known under the name of nana.

THE BOX

XXII

THE BOX

THE evergreen shrubs and small trees, popularly known as Boxes, are represented in gardens by not more than half a dozen species ; these are, however, augmented by a large number of varieties, the majority of which are of decorative value. Scientifically they are known by the generic name of Buxus, a genus belonging to the Spurge family, Euphorbiaceæ. The Boxes are recognised by their simple, leathery, opposite leaves which are destitute of stipules and have usually a clefted apex ; by their tiny, axillary, unisexual flowers, which are borne in small clusters in March, each cluster containing several male and one or two female flowers ; and by their three-celled fruits and black, nut-like seeds. The flowers are inconspicuous, and would almost escape notice were it not for the yellow anthers. The wood is very fine-grained and extremely hard. All the species here mentioned are found in the Northern Hemisphere, and belong to the Old World. Other species are known,

Holly, Yew and Box

but they are not in general cultivation. The hardy species are distributed as follows :—

Europe, N. Africa and W. Asia—
  B. sempervirens, *Linnæus*.
Balearic Islands, etc.—
  B. balearica, *Lambert*.
Himalaya—
  B. Wallichiana, *Bailley*.
China—
  B. Harlandi, *Hance*.
Japan—
  B. japonica, *Mueller*.

B. sempervirens—Description

This is the best known of the various hardy species and is widely distributed through Europe, N. Africa, and W. Asia. It is found wild in Britain on Box Hill, near Dorking, Surrey, but it is not certain that it is a native tree. The trees in that particular position have been there for a very long period, and references are made to them in some of the oldest gardening books. In *Trees of Commerce*, by *W. Stevenson*, reference is made to a lease of Box Hill, drawn up in August 1602, one of the clauses of which was, that "the tenant is commanded to use his best endeavours to preserve Yew, Box, and all other trees growing

COMMON BOX, BUXUS SEMPERVIRENS.   IN THE ROYAL GARDENS, KEW

The Box

thereupon, as also to deliver half-yearly an account of what hath been sold, to whom, and at what prices." In 1608 a number of trees were cut down upon the sheep walks on Box Hill, and the wood realised £50. The tree grows to a height of 15 or 20 feet, with a trunk diameter of 6 or 8 inches under ordinary conditions, but, in very favourable situations, these dimensions are exceeded. As a rule, a spreading head is formed, and the branches are thickly covered with small, oblong, or oval leaves. Like the Holly and Yew it thrives in a variety of soils and situations, and forms an excellent subject for undergrowth, as it succeeds in partial shade as well as in full sun. Although under normal conditions it attains the dimensions of a small tree, varieties are in cultivation which never grow more than a few feet in height, whilst one or two varieties hardly attain a height of 12 inches. Other varieties are recognised by means of variegated foliage.

Associations

As a hardy evergreen the Box has long occupied an important position in gardens, and in point of usefulness it closely approaches the Holly and the Yew. These three plants have in fact been associated for a very long period, and we find that in a cut state they have all been used

Holly, Yew and Box

for decorative purposes on the anniversaries of religious festivals. Although it is now the practice to use various popular evergreens indiscriminately for house and church decorations at various seasons, each one appears to have had its own particular period for use in the past, thus, whilst the Holly was undeniably the correct subject to use at Christmas time, and the Yew for Palm Sunday and Easter, the proper time to decorate with branches of Box was from Candlemas to Palm Sunday or Easter Eve.

Herrick refers to many of these old customs, and with reference to the Box says : " It was once a time-honoured custom on Candlemas-day to replace the Christmas evergreens with sprays of Box, which were kept up till Easter Eve, when they gave place to the Yew. This custom evidently gave rise to the following lines :—

> " Down with the Rosemary and Bays,
> Down with the Mistletoe ;
> Instead of Holly now upraise
> The greener Box for show."

It appears, however, to have been used in some places for Easter decorations, and has been assigned, with various other plants, the name of Palm, through Palm Sunday associations. Writers state that a custom prevails in some parts of France of decorating graves with Box on Palm Sunday. This custom may have arisen

The Box

on account of the symbolic meaning attributed to the plant by some old writers, *i.e.* "perpetual life in the other world." According to *Plant Lore* sprays of Box were used in conjunction with Woodruff, Lavender and Roses at one period, to decorate churches on the days dedicated to St Barnabas and St Paul.

In biblical history the Box figures on several occasions. The prophet *Isaiah, Chap. XLI., verse 19*, says, " I will set in the desert the Fir tree, and the Pine and the Box tree together." Again, in the *LX. Chap.*, the words occur in *verse* 13, " The glory of Lebanon shall come unto thee, the Fir tree, the Pine tree and the Box together, to beautify the place of my Sanctuary." Box wood, with many other woods, is credited with being the wood of which the cross for the Saviour's crucifixion was made (see *Plant Lore*).

As in the case of most of our common trees a number of curious legends and superstitions are attached to the Box. A custom at one time prevailed, and may do now, in some country districts, of using sprigs of Box in connection with funerals. A basin of Box sprays was placed at the door from which the coffin was carried, and each mourner was expected to take a piece, carry it with him to the churchyard, and throw it into the grave after the coffin had been lowered.

Holly, Yew and Box

Wordsworth alludes to this custom in the following lines :—

"The basin of Box-wood, just six months before,
Had stood on the table at Timothy's door.
A coffin through Timothy's threshold had passed,
One child did it bear, and that child was his last."

In *Plant Lore* we learn that it is a practice in Turkey with widows, who go weekly to pray at their husbands' graves, to plant a sprig of Box at the head of the grave. Among interesting items in the same work the following occur : "The evergreen Box, Buxus sempervirens, was specially consecrated by the Greeks to Pluto, the protector of all evergreen trees, as being symbolic of the life which continues through the winter, in the infernal regions, and in the other world." In connection with honey gathered from the flowers of the Box the following is related : "The ancients believed that the Box produced honey, and that in Trebizonde the honey issuing from this tree was so noxious that it drove men mad. Corsican honey was supposed to owe its ill-repute to the fact that the bees fed upon Box."

A pretty legend is recorded in relation to the monastery of St Christine in the Pyrenees. The arms of the monastery are those of the Knights of Christine, viz., a white pigeon with a cross in its beak, and the origin of its adoption is as follows: "The workmen who were employed

The Box

to build the monastery had the greatest difficulty
in finding a suitable foundation. After several
ineffectual attempts, they one morning perceived
a white pigeon flying with a cross in its beak.
They pursued the bird, which perched on a Box-
tree, but, though it flew away on their approach,
they found in the branches the cross which it had
left ; this they took to be a good omen, and proceeded successfully to lay the foundations on the
spot where the Box-tree had stood, and completed the edifice."

To believers in dreams it may be of interest to
learn that to dream of Box is considered to be a
fortunate occurrence, as it denotes long life and
prosperity, also a happy marriage.

From the *Treasury of Botany* we learn that
the "Common Box-tree" is the badge of the
clan M'Intosh, and its variegated variety that of
the M'Phersons.

XXIII

B. SEMPERVIRENS—*Continued*

Uses

ALTHOUGH in the British Isles the "Common Box" is used almost exclusively for decorative purposes, its timber forms in some countries a valuable article of commerce. The wood is very hard, smooth grained, and durable, and it has been used largely from the time of the ancients to the present date. In ancient times it was used for ornamental boxes and inlaid with ivory. It has been thought to be the Ashur wood of scripture, and as such was used with inlaying of ivory in the decorative splendour of Tyre (*see Plant Lore*). In more modern times its greatest use has been for blocks for wood engravings, whilst it has also been used for cabinet-making, mathematical instruments, handles of tools, combs, rulers, walking-sticks, and many other things. Evelyn refers to the use of the wood as follows : " The turner, engraver, carver, mathematical instrument, comb and pipe makers, give

B. sempervirens

great prices for it by weight as well as measure, and by the seasoning and divers manners of cutting vigorous insolations, politure and grinding, the roots of this tree (as even our common and neglected Thorn) do furnish the inlayers and cabinet-makers with pieces rarely undulated, and full of variety. Also of Box are made wheels or shivers (as our ship carpenters call them) and pins for blocks and pulleys, pegs for musical instruments, nutcrackers, weavers' shuttles, hollar-sticks, bump-sticks, and dressers for the shoe-makers, rulers, rolling-pins, pestles, mall-balls, beetles, tops, tables, chess-men, screws male and female, bobbins for bone-lace, spoons, nay, the stoutest axle-trees above all."

With reference to the making of combs from the wood for ladies' use Evelyn gives the following lines :—

> " Box-combs bear no small part
> In the *Militia* of the *Female Art;*
> They tye the *links* which hold our *Gallants* fast
> And spread the *Nets* to which fond *Lovers* hast."

Although other woods are now used in wood engraving, the Box is still employed for the best class work, and the principal source of production is the neighbourhood of the Black Sea. The supply is, however, becoming short, and is not likely to be increased rapidly, as the growth of the Box is very slow. The *Diplomatic and*

Holly, Yew and Box

Consular Report, No. 1371, published in 1894, dealing with the trade of Batoum, reports on Box-wood on page 29 as follows: "In the accessible private forests the Box-wood has been mostly cut down, the Government wisely does not desire that their forests shall in a few years be cleared of wood that takes hundreds of years to mature, and place but little on the market. But substitutes from other parts of the world are taking the place of Box-wood." In Report No. 1717, published in 1895, further mention is made of this wood as follows: "The export of timber has been far from satisfactory, and the only trade of importance has been done in Box-wood and Walnut." Reference is made to the condition of the Box forests in the following words: "Although all the private forests of Box-wood have been exhausted the Government up to the present still refuse to sell or allow Box-wood to be cut in their extensive forests throughout Abkhasia, consequently the total exports from the Caucasus have not exceeded 1200 tons; and further, this wood is fast losing its importance to the English manufacturers, owing to the fact that in recent years other hard woods have been discovered which are equally suitable for making many articles for which Box-wood was formerly used. Besides this, Box-wood from other countries also finds its way to the English market in increasing quantities."

B. sempervirens

According to these reports, the Box-wood exported from the Port of Poti was :—

In 1890, 600 tons, valued at £5000

,, 1891, 60 ,,   ,,   ,,   400

,, 1894, 424 ,,   ,,   ,,   4240

,, 1895, 54 ,,   ,,   ,,   540

Most of the Box-wood that finds its way into the London markets is said to come via Turkey or Odessa, even if procured from distant countries. *Herbert Stone*, F.L.S., in his book on *Timbers of Commerce and their Identification*, says that Russian Box-wood is rapidly being replaced by West Indian Box-wood, except for the very best articles, on account of its increasing cost.

The *Diplomatic and Consular Report, No.* 3864, states that in 1906, 3,500,000 lbs. of Box-wood was exported from the Mazanderan (Persia) forests, to Russia.

Loudon gives a lot of interesting information about Box-wood in *Arb. Frutic.* In speaking of the growth and use of the wood in France, he says : " The wood of trunks in France is rarely found of sufficient size for blocks, and where it is, it is so dear that trees are not cut down at once, but pieces are taken from living trees as required." In his time the French turners were wont to place the wood in dark cellars for a period of from three to five years, to keep it from splitting. It was then taken out, the bark removed, and buried in the ground to keep it from the light until required for use. He also states that in 1815 trees on Box-hill to the cost of £10,000 were cut down. The earliest specimen of wood engraving in England now extant is said to be in the collection of Earl Spencer, and represents St Christopher carrying the infant Saviour; it dates back to 1423. In addition to Box-trees being found in quantity about the neighbourhood of the Black Sea, they are said to be plentiful in the forests in Franche Compté, Dauphiné, Haute Provence, and the chain of mountains stretching across Languedoc and the Pyrenees.

Dryden makes one or two references to the use of Box-wood as follows :—

> " The Beech, the swimming Alder and the Plane,
> Hard Box and Linden of a softer grain."

And also :—

> " Nor Box nor Limes without their use ;
> Smooth-grain'd and proper for the turner's trade,
> Which curious hands may carve, and steel with ease
> invade."   —*Dryden's Virgil.*

Decorative Uses

In the British Isles the Boxes are planted solely for decorative purposes, and, though they attain their greatest size on rich loamy soil, they thrive well on heavy soil and in that of a poor sandy character. The adaptability of the

B. sempervirens

"Common Box" for poor soils seems to have been known to Pope, for he writes :—

"Waste sandy valleys once perplex'd with Thorn,
The spiny Fir and shapely Box adorn."

For groups in the wilder parts of the garden the tall growing forms are well fitted, whilst varieties with pendulous branches form handsome lawn specimens. The dwarfer varieties are of value for beds or groups in shrubberies, whilst the same may be said of the varieties with variegated leaves. For planting beneath the shade of trees and in dark corners they are excellent, whilst for a position facing north, where no sunshine is obtainable, few plants thrive better. A dwarf form known as suffruticosa is used extensively for planting as an edging to paths, and no shrub is neater if kept well clipped. When the severe style of geometrical gardening existed, this Box was of great service for marking out the beds.

In the sixteenth and seventeenth centuries, when topiary work was so much in vogue, the compact growing varieties were eagerly sought after for clipping into fantastic shapes, their small leaves and dense habit peculiarly fitting them for the purpose. Even in the present day a few people try to revive topiary work, and varieties of Box are largely used for the purpose. Pliny is said to have described his Tusculan villa as having "a

221

Holly, Yew and Box

lawn adorned with figures of animals cut out in Box trees, answering alternately to one another. This lawn was again surrounded by a walk enclosed with evergreen shrubs, sheared into a variety of forms. Beyond this was a place of exercise, of a circular form, ornamented in the middle with Box trees, sheared, as before, into numerous different figures ; and the whole fenced in by a sloping bank covered with Box rising in steps to the top." In another part of the grounds attached to the villa the Box is mentioned as being cut into a variety of shapes and letters, some expressing the name of the master, and others that of the artificer, etc.

With reference to a Topiary Garden, *Loudon* quotes the following lines by *G. West:*—

> " There likewise mote be seen on every side
> The shapely Box, of all its branching pride
> Ungently shorn, and with preposterous skill,
> To various beasts, and birds of sundry quill
> Transform'd, and human shapes of monstrous size.
>
> .   .   .   .   .
>
> Also other wonders of the sportive shears,
> Fair Nature misadorning, there are found ;
> Globes, spiral columns, pyramids and piers
> With spouting urns and budding statues crown'd ;
> And horizontal dials on the ground,
> In living Box, by cunning artists traced ;
> And galleys trim, on no long voyage bound,
> But by their roots there ever anchor'd fast."

The upright growing sorts are sometimes used

B. sempervirens

for hedges, but they are not employed to any great extent. A Box hedge is neither so strong or so ornamental as either the Yew or the Holly, and is not to be recommended except in cases where it is required simply as a dividing line or low wind-break.

Propagation

Propagation is usually effected by means of cuttings of young shoots 3 or 4 inches long placed in sandy soil under a handlight in summer. These root in a few weeks' time, and may then be transferred to the nursery border. Growth for the first three or four years is slow, but in the case of the stronger-growing varieties it becomes more rapid afterwards.

XXIV

B. SEMPERVIRENS—*Continued*

Varieties

B. **S. arborescens.** — This name is applied to the largest growing form of the "Common Box," which is really typical of the species as found growing under the most suitable conditions. The leaves are of normal size, but vary somewhat on different plants. They usually range from ¾ of an inch to 1 inch in length, and from ¼ to ½ an inch in width. Specimens may produce several trunks from near the ground line, or they may form single trunks only. Mature specimens, if not crowded by other plants, develop large heads, and are equally ornamental, whether clothed to the ground with branches or with a portion of the trunk exposed to view.

B. s. argentea = argenteo - marginata. — A dense, but not stiff, growing variety, with normal sized leaves. It is distinguished by its leaves being margined with silver. The variegation is not equally developed, sometimes being confined to a narrow border, or again taking up the greater portion of the leaf. As a rule the variegation is more noticeable about the apex than the base.

B. sempervirens

B. s. aureo-maculata.—This variety is recognised by its loose and graceful habit, and by its leaves being blotched and striated with gold. As the leaves advance in age much of the colour is lost, but in the case of those up to one year old it occupies about half the space. It belongs to the large-growing section.

B. s. aurea pendula = "Golden Weeping Box."— A very ornamental sort, distinguished from the last-named by the pendulous habit of the secondary branches. The leaves are about ¾ of an inch long and barely ⅓ of an inch wide. The golden colouring in some instances is confined to narrow margins, whilst at others it occupies the greater part of the surface. It grows into a good-sized bush.

B. s. aureo-marginata. — This is a strong-growing variety of rather stiff, upright habit, with broadly-oval leaves which sometimes have a curious way of narrowing rapidly near the apex, at other times being quite rounded, or again undulated and malformed. The disk is deep green, and the variegation is in the form of an irregular golden band. It is not one of the most desirable sorts.

B. s. elegantissima.—Where a neat-growing, silver-variegated evergreen is required, this might well be tried. It is a slow-growing sort of upright habit, with rather small and narrow leaves, many of which are deformed. The variegation is conspicuously developed; sometimes on the youngest growths, occupying the greater part of the leaf surface, and usually forming a wide marginal band. Shapely specimens are formed without pruning, whilst it is possible by cutting it back once a year to keep it in a very dwarf state without making it look bare.

B. s. Handsworthii.—A strong-growing variety of dense, upright habit, with bold, broadly-oval leaves of a dark green colour. It is inclined to form a wide bush rather than assume a tree-like habit. Its vigorous growth fits it well for hedge work, and serviceable hedges 4 feet high can be obtained by using it for the purpose.

B. s. latifolia.—This is a stiff-growing sort of rather fastigiate habit, with very large, broadly-oval leaves. The largest leaves exceed 1 inch in length and are ¾ of an inch wide. They are very deep green in colour. Its stiff habit fits it for hedge work, whilst it is sometimes grown as formal pyramids in tubs for various kinds of decorative work where tender plants would be inappropriate. For ornamental gardening it is less useful than the free-habited sorts.

B. s. latifolia bullata.—A form of the last-named with a somewhat dwarfer habit and shorter leaves. Like the former plant, it has deep green foliage.

B. s. latifolia macrophylla.—In point of size of leaf there is little to be seen between this and

B. sempervirens

typical latifolia. The habit is, however, somewhat looser, and the leaves rather lighter
coloured.

B. s. latifolia maculata. — The habit of the
plant and the size of the leaves are similar to
B. latifolia, but the leaves are blotched and
striped with gold. The variegation is not, however, very conspicuous.

B. s. longifolia.—A dense growing variety of
upright habit, with deep green leaves. It is
chiefly remarkable for its long and comparatively
narrow foliage. The largest leaves are nearly
$1\frac{1}{2}$ inches long and barely half an inch in width.
It is a bushy variety, and does not look as if it
will grow to any great size; possibly 6 or 8 feet
high only.

B. s. myosotifolia = " Forget - me - not - leaved
Box."—This is a very distinct and pretty dwarf
growing sort with green leaves. It is of dense
habit, forming a compact mass, and increasing
very slowly in height. Plants 10 or 12 years
of age rarely exceed a foot in height. The larger
leaves are $\frac{1}{2}$ an inch long and $\frac{1}{8}$ inch wide, whilst
some are considerably smaller.

B. s. myrtifolia = B. myrtifolia, B. s. leptophylla and "Myrtle-leaved Box."—An excellent
variety of dwarf habit, with small green leaves.
It is of slow growth, but rises to a height of 4 or
5 feet under favourable conditions; the habit,
though upright, being relieved from stiffness.

P   227

Holly, Yew and Box

The leaves are similar in shape to those of the last-mentioned variety, but a trifle larger.

B. s. pendula.—This is without doubt one of the very best evergreens we possess. It attains tree-like proportions, forming a distinct trunk with an upright leading shoot. The secondary branches are pendulous, and the whole tree is of very graceful outline. Fine specimens of it may be seen in the neighbourhood of the ruinous arch at Kew. Another pendulous variety is known with rather large leaves and stronger branches, it also is very ornamental. Both are green-leaved varieties.

B. s. prostrata.—The principal peculiarity of this green-leaved variety lies in the horizontal growth of the branches. It never attains a height of more than a few feet, but covers a considerable area of ground.

B. s. pyramidalis. — This variety is distinguished by its stiff, pyramidal habit and formal outline. It is a green-leaved variety, and is used to some extent for topiary work ; for ordinary decorative gardening it is not commendable.

B. s. rosmarinifolia = B. rosmarinifolius, B. thymifolia, and " Rosemary-leaved Box."—An elegant habited variety, with small, dark green leaves. It forms a shapely bush several feet high of graceful outline, and does not quickly outgrow its position. For topiary work, it was at one time used extensively.

B. sempervirens

B. s. salicifolia elata = "Willow-leaved Box."
—In this variety the leaves are about 1 inch or
1¼ inches long, barely ⅓ of an inch wide, and
green in colour.   The plant is of upright growth,
but is not at all stiff.   Where variety is required it
is a good sort to plant.

B. s. suffruticosa = B. suffruticosa and "Edging
Box."—This is a well-known dwarf variety, being
used in almost every garden of any size in the
country for edging purposes.   For this purpose
it has been used for a very long period, and
when the severe geometrical style of gardening
was in vogue a couple of centuries ago, it was
used to work out elaborate designs for parterres,
the interspaces being filled in with different
coloured sand, gravel, stones, or what not.

B. s. undulifolia. — A strong-growing sort,
differing little from the type except by the
undulating margins of the leaves.

Other Species

B. balearica, *Lambert* = sempervirens gigantea.
—This is a large-growing species of tree-like
habit found in Minorca, Sardinia, Corsica, and
European and Asiatic Turkey.   It was first introduced into France in 1770, and from thence
was received in England ten years later.   On its
introduction it was treated as a greenhouse plant,
but there is no necessity to question its hardiness,

229

Holly, Yew and Box

for examples are to be found which have withstood the severest winters experienced in England during the last fifty years. The tree, under favourable conditions, attains a height of 70 or 80 feet, with a trunk 2 feet in diameter ; in England, however, it forms but a small tree or large bush. The leaves are larger than those of other Boxes, being from 1½ to 2 inches long and ¾ to nearly an inch in width. They are of a rich green colour, and thick and coriaceous in texture. The bark of the young wood is green, whilst that of the trunk and older branches is grey and deeply marked. The wood is used for purposes similar to those for which the wood of the " Common Box " is of value, but it is said to be coarser and less valuable. Large quantities are stated to be exported from Constantinople. An illustration is given of a specimen of this species growing at Kew. Over sixty years ago Loudon mentions this specimen as being 13 feet high and the largest within ten miles of London ; it is now 22½ feet in height, with a girth near the ground of 3 feet 3 inches, and at 3 feet above the ground 2 feet 5½ inches. A fine example, 12 feet high and as far through, may be seen in the ground at Ashton Court, Bristol.

B. Harlandi, *Hance.* — A species sometimes met with in gardens under the name of B. chinensis. The latter name is, however, a synonym of Simmondsia californica. B. Har-

BUXUS BALEARICA IN THE ROYAL GARDENS, KEW

B. sempervirens

landi is a native of China, and under cultivation forms a small, upright habited bush, with rather bright green leaves 1¼ to 1½ inches long and barely a quarter of an inch wide. It is of service where a small, neat growing evergreen is desired, but should not be placed in a position where a plant is required at least 2 feet high, for it takes many years to attain that height.

B. japonica, *Mueller.*—This plant differs from the other Boxes by its light green obovate or almost round leaves. It is of rather loose habit, and the leafage is not so dense as in most sorts. The angled nature of the branches, conspicuous in all Boxes, is very pronounced in this species, the angles being almost winged. Although a free-growing plant, it does not grow more than a few feet in height. It is a native of Japan.

B. j. microphylla = B. microphylla.—A small-leaved form of the above plant.

B. Wallichiana, *Bailley.*—A very rare, strong growing species, conspicuous for its long, narrow leaves. These are from 1¾ to 2½ inches in length, and barely ½ an inch in width. As in the case of B. balearica it forms a very ornamental plant, but it is less frequently met with, probably on account of its being a difficult species to propagate. It is a native of the Himalaya.

OTHER EVERGREENS

XXV

THE HARDY HEATHS

ALTHOUGH it is impossible to cultivate the various hardy Heaths without a great deal of expense and trouble in some parts of the country, they are indispensable for every well-appointed garden, situated in those places where peat-loving plants thrive. For the colder parts of the country some sorts are undesirable on account of hardiness; there are, however, others that are perfectly strong enough to withstand the severest winters in any part of the British Isles. Their unsuitability for various districts is wholly on account of soil and water. With a few exceptions the members of the Heath, or giving it its correct name, Erica, family detest lime, and refuse to thrive in soil impregnated with it to any serious extent, whilst they are also very impatient of water which contains lime in quantity. Essentially peat-loving plants, they are found in the greatest luxuriance on light or peaty soil, the British species attaining their greatest perfection on wide, open moorlands and hillsides, where the soil is sweet and open and the atmosphere pure. It must not, however, be inferred that it is impossible to cultivate the various sections of the great family in any but peaty soil, for very satisfactory results are obtained in moderately heavy loam, providing lime is absent, or present in minute quantities only.

All the species suitable for outdoor culture in the British Isles are of European origin, for although in a few of the warmer parts of the country South African species have been tried, they have not proved an unqualified success. Some of the most beautiful of the European species are found growing naturally in Spain and Portugal, consequently they are unsuitable for cold districts ; they, however, grow admirably in the southern and western counties, and are also a success in some parts of the midlands. It may safely be assumed that they will withstand from 15 to 18 degrees *Fahr.* of frost without injury, providing that temperature is not extended over a longer period than two or three days ; but if the temperature becomes lower, and no steps are taken to provide protection, death or serious injury is the result. About London the more tender species have stood without injury through the last twelve winters ; the severe winter of 1894-5, however, proved fatal to many. On the arrival of severe frost it is a good plan to sprinkle a quantity of dry leaves about the lower parts of the branches, and a little Bracken or other protective material amongst the upper parts.

When preparing ground for Heaths it should be dug over to a depth of at least 18 inches. If of a peaty nature the natural soil will of course do, if not it should be made as light as possible, adding sand if the natural ground is heavy. After the digging, a layer of peat 6 inches deep should be spread over the ground and be lightly forked in, this will be found preferable to removing a foot or more of soil and filling up the space with peat. In lime districts it will be necessary to remove the whole of the soil to a depth of 2 feet, and fill up the excavation with imported material. Even in such a case as this it is inadvisable to provide a great depth of peat, rather fill in with light soil and give a surfacing of peat. A great bulk of peat decomposes and becomes sour before roots can push their way through it, whereas ordinary light, loamy soil keeps sweet. At Kew numerous large masses of Heaths have been formed, and these are thriving well in the ordinary Kew sand with a few inches of peat.

When planting, advantage should be taken of the fact that the species are divided into spring and autumn flowering groups ; by planting each lot separately very fine effects are produced. Possibly no other genera provides such a lengthy display of flower, for, although the normal time for the flowers of some spring forms to appear is February, they often begin to open during the previous November, whilst blossoms are still to be found in quantity in May. The autumn flowering set, likewise, commence to bloom in summer, are at their best during early autumn, and continue to bear flowers until November. With cultivated Heaths it is a good plan to go over the plants after the flowers have faded and cut away the old flower heads; this results in more compact plants, whilst they last in good health for a longer period if not allowed to perfect their seeds.

Propagation is effected by means of layers or by cuttings. The latter is by far the better method, and produces the best plants. Cuttings of young shoots are taken during July, August, and September, and dibbled into firm, peaty soil, either in pots or under handlights out-of-doors. If placed in pots they should be stood in a close propagating case in a little heat until roots are formed, which will be in about six weeks' time. The pots should then be stood in an open moist greenhouse, near the glass, to harden off, and the young plants be eventually transferred to a sheltered border in the nursery. Cuttings placed under handlights should be left undisturbed until the following May, when they may be transferred to a bed in the nursery. Layers may be put

The Hardy Heaths

down any time during spring and summer. Large, spreading plants are selected, and a little peaty soil is placed under the branches; the branches are then weighted down into the soil by means of stones. A period of twelve months has to elapse before the layers are sufficiently well rooted to be detached from the parent.

Selection of Species

E. arborea = "The Tree Heath." — A handsome plant of upright, bushy habit, found in the region bordering the Mediterranean and also in the Caucasus. Under favourable conditions it attains a height of from 12 to 20 feet, but is more frequently met with from 4 to 8 feet high. The flowers are small, fragrant, and white, and borne in great profusion from March to May. There is a dwarf variety called alpina, but it is of little value.

E. australis is found in Portugal, and is recognised by a rather loose, straggling habit, dark green leaves, and red flowers, which are larger than those of most Heaths. It has been in cultivation since 1769, but is not a well known plant.

E. carnea.—This is widely distributed through the mountainous regions of Europe, and is recognised by its dwarf, compact, carpet-like appearance, rarely exceeding 6 or 8 inches in height. The flowers are red, and borne from February to May. The variety alba is recognised by its white flowers. E. herbacea is a synonym of this species.

E. ciliaris is widely distributed through South-western Europe, and occurs in Cornwall and other of the warmer counties. It is of weak, wiry growth, has curious ciliated leaves, and bears terminal inflorescences of red flowers from July to October. The variety Mawiana is a native of Portugal, and is one of the most decorative of our autumn-flowering Heaths. It is of more compact growth than the type, and bears larger and more upright racemes of deeper coloured flowers. The blossoming period is from July to November.

E. cinerea.—During August and September many thousands of acres of moorland in the British Isles are made beautiful by the blossoms of this Heath, whilst the same may be said of it throughout the greater part of Western and Central Europe. The type grows from 6 inches to a foot in height, and bears reddish-purple flowers. It is, however, a variable plant, and flowers of various colours are to be found. A number of distinct forms have been selected for varietal names, some of the best being alba and alba minor, white; purpurea and atropurpurea, purple; atrosanguinea, deep red; coccinea, bright red; rosea, rose; and polypetala, red, with petals divided into many segments.

E. lusitanica = codonodes and polytrichifolia. —This, like arborea and australis, is one of the more tender species, but thrives about London. It is an extremely handsome plant, the branches being upright and plumose and the leaves a delightful shade of green. The flowers are pink in bud and white when expanded, and they are at their best from March to May. It is a native of Spain and Portugal.

E. Mackaii = Mackaiana and Tetralix Mackayana.—This is considered to be a natural hybrid between E. ciliaris and E. Tetralix, the habit being intermediate between the two; the leaves most closely resemble those of the former plant and the flowers the latter. It has been found in Spain, and also in Ireland.

E. mediterranea. — Although slightly tender this is an extremely useful and ornamental Heath. It is found in South-west France and Spain, and under favourable conditions attains a height of 15 feet. More frequently it is met with from 2 to 5 feet high, forming dense bushes. The flowers are pink and borne from early March to May. There is a form of it found in Ireland, which is given the varietal name of hibernica. Other varieties are alba, glauca, nana, and hybrida. The latter is a natural hybrid between mediterranea and carnea,

Holly, Yew and Box

and is one of the best flowering plants we possess, the reddish flowers commencing to open in November, whilst they are at their best about the end of February, and last in first-rate condition until May.

E. multiflora = peduncularis in part.—This is one of the autumn-flowering set, and is recognised by reason of its very floriferous habit and reddish flowers. It is a native of S. Europe and closely resembles E. vagans.

E. stricta. — Although some botanists say that this plant is strictly E. terminalis, it is doubtful whether it will lose the former name for garden purposes. Although by some people it is considered somewhat tender, it grows without injury at an elevation of 1100 feet in Derbyshire. The flowers are reddish in colour and borne during autumn. It grows 5 or 6 feet in height and is a native of S. Europe. Among its synonyms the following are numbered —corsica, multicaulis, pendula, and ramulosa.

E. Tetralix = "Cross-leaved Heath." — This is widely distributed through Europe and is common in Britain. It is recognised by the curious angled arrangement of its leaves, and upright, terminal heads of deep pink or reddish flowers. There are varieties—alba, mollis, and rubra.

E. vagans = "Cornish Heath."—In some parts of Cornwall this plant covers a large area of ground, though it appears to inhabit the more southern parts only. It is a very ornamental, autumn - flowering species, bearing pinkish blossoms in profusion. The variety alba has white flowers, whilst grandiflora and rubra produce reddish blooms.

E. Veitchii.—Five or six years ago this useful Heath was introduced to our gardens by Mr Veitch of Exeter. It is a hybrid between arborea and lusitanica, and partakes of the good qualities of both, being of good habit and exceedingly floriferous. The flowers are white and borne from March to May.

E. Watsoni = Tetralici-ciliaris.—This is probably a natural hybrid between E. Tetralia and E. ciliaris. It is of loose habit, bears red flowers during late summer, and was found in South-western England.

Near Allies of the Heaths

A number of genera exist, consisting of one or two evergreen species each, which belong to the natural order Ericaceæ, and require similar culture to the Ericas. The most important are referred to below.

Calluna

The only species of this genus is C. vulgaris, the " Ling " of our moors, commons, and mountain sides. It is recognised by its three-cornered leaves, which are arranged in a curiously angled manner on the stems, and its upright, terminal racemes of reddish-purple flowers, which are borne during autumn. It varies considerably in habit, sometimes rising to a height of 5 or 6 feet, and sometimes bearing a resemblance to a dwarf, compact moss, with all sorts of intermediate stages. The colour of the flowers also varies, and for these two reasons a selection of some of the most distinct has been made, to which varietal names have been given. Of these, good ones are alba, alba minor, alba pilosa, alba Serlei, alba tenella, and Hammondi, with white flowers; aurea and cuprea, with golden leaves; Alporti, rosea, and rubra, with red flowers; flore pleno, with double flowers; and hypnoides, minima, Foxii, and pygmaea, of dwarf, moss-like appearance.

Dabœcia

D. polifolia, the "St Dabeoc's Heath," is the only species of this genus. It is a very floriferous, low-growing shrub, with upright racemes of drooping, urn-shaped, red flowers. Varieties are known with white, and red and white flowers mixed.

Bryanthus. — This is a Heath - like genus, containing but a few species of dwarf shrubs,

The Hardy Heaths

with pretty, usually red flowers. All are rare and choice plants, requiring similar treatment to the Heaths. The species are Breweri, empetriformis, and taxifolius. A fourth plant, B. erectus, is known. This is a hybrid between B. empetriformis and Rhodothamnus Chamæcistus.

Rhodothamnus chamæcistus.—A pretty, dwarf, Rhododendron-like shrub, which rarely exceeds a foot in height. It bears pretty flowers, heavily flushed with rose on a white ground. Unlike most Ericaceous plants it likes lime.

Bruckenthalia spiculifolia is a charming, dwarf, Heath-like plant from Eastern Europe and Asia Minor. The leaves are a deep shade of green and the flowers are white, slightly flushed with pink, borne in short, upright racemes.

Leiophyllum buxifolium. — This is the "Sand Myrtle" of the United States. It is a pleasing little shrub, a foot or so high, with tiny, Box-like leaves, and white, rose-flushed flowers. If cultivated with the Heaths it will be a success.

XXVI

THE BAMBOOS, ETC.

THOUGH fifteen years ago it was the exception rather than the rule to find Bamboo representatives in gardens, so popular have they become in the meantime that it is almost impossible to find a really good garden without a collection. Popular though as they are, Bamboos are not things to plant indiscriminately, especially in exposed places, for they suffer badly from cold winds, worse even than from frost. When at their best they are, without doubt, the most graceful of all evergreen shrubs, and from July until February they hold their own with anything we have. Unfortunately, however, from February onwards, for several months, Bamboos as a rule are decidedly untidy, many of the old leaves being brown and retained on the plants until the appearance of young ones, which are not at their best until the end of June. For this reason it is advisable to form a small garden for Bamboos and kindred plants, and keep them together rather than place them indiscriminately amongst other shrubs. As Bamboos are essentially water-

The Bamboos

loving subjects, care should be taken to place them in naturally damp ground or in such a place that a good supply of water can be obtained without trouble during dry weather. The kind of soil required for Bamboo culture is not very particular, providing it is made moderately rich, light and heavy loams all being suitable. The ground should be well trenched previous to planting, and if poor it should be enriched by an addition of well decayed manure and leaves. The most suitable time to plant is May, particularly if the material consists of pieces severed from old stocks. As soon as the work is completed a good watering should be given, and care must be taken to ensure frequent watering should the weather prove to be at all dry. When once clumps are well established, an annual top-dressing in April or May will be found to be of great service. About February or March each year the clumps should be gone over and all canes removed right down to the base that show signs of being worn out. It is highly essential that these canes should be removed to the base, for if left a few inches in length they will choke the young shoots. Clumps that have become very large may be improved by being divided up in May. This division of the stools encourages a greater number of vigorous young shoots.

Propagation is usually effected by division of the clumps, though, when seeds can be obtained,

Holly, Yew and Box

they are preferable. The flowering of Bamboos has occasioned much uneasiness amongst garden lovers of late years, for after Bamboos flower they usually die. When a clump flowers it is advisable to keep a sharp look-out for seeds, for if young seedling plants are obtained it is safe to say that they will not bloom for at least thirty years.

The hardy Bamboos are included in three genera—Bambusa, Arundinaria, and Phyllostachys. The majority of the hardiest are natives of China and Japan, but one comes from N. America. For the warmer counties a few Indian species are available, but they are of no value for out-door culture in other parts. In stature, hardy Bamboos can be obtained from a foot in height to quite 20 feet or more; whilst some form large carpet-like masses, others imposing groups of upright shoots, and others clumps of gracefully arched branches.

Suitable species for general culture are as follows.

Sorts which grow from 1 to 4 feet in height:—

Arundinaria

auricoma, chrysantha, Fortunei, humilis, pumila, pygmæa, Veitchii.

Bambusa

disticha, tessellata.

The Bamboos

Phyllostachys

ruscifolia.

Taller growing species :—

Arundinaria

anceps, Hindsii, and the variety graminea, japonica, Kokantsik, Kumassasa, macrosperma, nitida, Simoni.

Phyllostachys

aurea, fastuosa, Henonis, mitis, nigra and varieties Boryana and punctata, Quilioi, Castillonis, viridiglaucescens.

Twelve of the most ornamental species and varieties :—

Arundinaria

nitida, Simoni, japonica (Metake), Hindsii var graminea, Kumassasa, anceps.

Phyllostachys

fastuosa, flexuosa, Henonis, nigra, Castillonis, viridi-glaucescens.

The Strawberry-trees (*Arbutus*)

The accompanying illustration gives some idea of the effect produced by a group of Arbutus, but it fails to bring to light all that is of decorative use about the trees. For instance, the effect is greatly enhanced when almost every branch is terminated by a panicle of white or pinkish flowers ; or at another period when the orange and scarlet, Strawberry-like fruits are ripe ; but even these do not exhaust the interesting features of the trees, for several possess the peculiar habit of casting off their old bark each year, and the quaint appearance of old and new bark always attracts attention.

The majority are of European origin, but one species hails from America. All thrive in light peaty soil, or, in fact, any lightish ground that does not contain lime in any appreciable quantity. They are increased by means of seeds or layers and some of the varieties by grafting on to stocks of A. Unedo. It is advisable to place them in permanent quarters early in life, as they transplant badly after they have attained a height of 4 or 5 feet, without considerable trouble is taken to remove a large ball of soil attached to the roots.

The chief sorts are :—

A. Andrachne. — A small tree which sometimes attains a height of 30 feet, found in the Levant and other places in the vicinity. The leaves are oblong, blunt and entire, and sometimes measure 6 inches in length, the flowers being greenish white and borne in upright

GROUP OF STRAWBERRY TREES (ARBUTUS SPECIES)

The Strawberry-trees

panicles during early spring. The old bark peels off during autumn and winter.

A. hybrida. — This is a hybrid between A. Andrachne and A. Unedo. It is intermediate in habit between the two ; the leaves are, however, less blunt and the margins are serrated. The bark peels off, but not so much as in A. Andrachne.

A. Menziesii.—A rare species from California, rather tender when young. It resembles A. Andrachne to some extent but has larger leaves, the margins of which are often finely serrated. When young, growth is very rapid, and as it continues to grow late in the year the points become badly ripened, hence its tender character. The old bark peels off in large flakes. A large specimen may be seen at Kew.

A. Unedo.—This is the "Common Strawberry-tree," a tree included in the British Flora, for it is found wild in the neighbourhood of Killarney. In Ireland it forms portions of woods in some places, and where drawn up it assumes tree-like proportions with good sized trunks ; it is, however, more frequently met with in the form of large dense bushes when grown in gardens, and as such is decidedly handsome, whether used as lawn specimens or groups in the wilder parts. The leaves are more or less elliptical, with serrated margins, and are up to 4 inches in length and 2 inches in width. The

Holly, Yew and Box

flowers are borne in terminal panicles during October and November, and are whitish in colour. An ornamental variety is in commerce known as rubra, or sometimes called Croomii; this has reddish flowers. Other varieties are compacta, integerrima, microphylla, and quercifolia.

The Rhododendrons

For places where Rhododendrons thrive the genus Rhododendron opens up a wide field for selection, for not only are many of them excellent evergreens, but they are also the most gorgeous of flowering shrubs. In the genus material may be found for all sorts of sites and conditions, for we find some which rarely rise more than a foot or so above the ground, whilst there are others which attain almost tree-like dimensions. Then, very many are eminently suited for the most conspicuous place that can be allotted them, whilst others form an excellent undergrowth for thin woods. The common R. ponticum, when allowed to grow freely, forms an immense bush 12 to 18 feet high, and proves an excellent block to shut out unsightly objects, whilst if cut over occasionally it forms an ideal cover plant. A charming feature can be made by grouping together many of the small-growing species, whilst the larger growing ones and the

The Rhododendrons

many garden varieties are well fitted for planting together in beds or masses to provide a special feature. Although there is a very wide selection for the greater part of the country, the warmer counties have a still larger number to select from, for there are many species from the Himalaya and China that are scarcely hardy enough for outdoor work except in those counties.

To succeed with Rhododendrons it is necessary to provide sweet soil free from lime or containing lime in minute quantities only. Peaty soil is that most suited to their requirements, though they grow well in loamy soil if lime is absent. Though it is not essential that shade should be provided, it is better if a position can be given where shade from midday sun is gained. An ideal position for Rhododendrons is a cool, moist but well drained valley sheltered from cold winds and where mists are plentiful. If peat does not form the natural soil it should not be introduced in large quantities, a little placed about the roots, mixed with the natural soil, being more suitable than a greater bulk. When planting, great care should be taken not to cover the top roots with more than half an inch of soil, and it is even better to cover with a layer of decayed leaves, if obtainable, than with soil. Rhododendrons give little trouble in the way of pruning, for they rarely require more than the removal of the old flower heads as soon as the flowers have fallen.

Propagation may be effected in any of the following ways:—Seeds, cuttings, grafts, or layers. The former method is only adopted in the case of new sorts and rare species, as it is a very slow way of obtaining plants. Cuttings are used in the case of the smaller growing sorts; grafts are used for most of the garden varieties, and layers for almost any sort. The latter method will be found to be the most suitable one for the inexperienced propagator.

Small growing sorts :—indicum amœnum, ledifolium, caucasicum, cinnabarinum (sometimes tall), ferrugineum (will grow in limy soil), arbutifolium, Wilsoni, glaucum, halense, ponticum cheiranthifolium, p. daphnoides, p. lancifolium, præcox, punctatum, racemosum, rubiginosum, Smirnowi, Smithii aureum, Broughtoni aureum, venustum, yunnanense, azaleoides, gemmiferum, Gowenianum.

Tall growing species for general culture :—californicum, campanulatum, catawbiense, Fortunei, maximum, ponticum, Thomsoni.

First hybrids, tall growing section :—altaclerense, Blandianum, kewense, Luscombei, Manglesii, Nobleanum, pulcherrimum, Russellianum, Smithii album.

Select list of garden varieties :—Alexander Dancer, rose; Amphion, pink; album grandi-

The Rhododendrons

florum, white; Baroness Lionel Rothschild, crimson; Baron Schroder, plum, yellow centre; Broughtonii, rosy crimson; Caractacus, crimson; Chas. Bagley, bright red; Duchess of Bedford, crimson; Duchess of Connaught, white, lemon marks; Earl of Shannon, crimson; fastuosum fl. pl., semi-double lilac; Frederick Waterer, bright crimson; Gomer Waterer, white; John Waterer, crimson; Kate Waterer, rosy crimson, yellow mark; Lady Clementine Mitford, pink; Lady Godiva, white; Madame Carvalho, white; Michael Waterer, crimson; Mrs A. Waterer, white, blotched; Mrs Agnew, white, lemon blotch; Mrs W. Agnew, rose; Mrs Holford, rose; Pink Pearl, pink; Princess Mary of Cambridge, white, rose edge; Queen, white; Strategist, pale pink.

XXVII

THE EVERGREEN OAKS AND IVIES

SEVERAL species of the genus Quercus, the scientific name under which the various oaks are included, form a distinct group by reason of their evergreen leaves. They are well suited for decorative gardening in the warmer parts of the country, but it is inadvisable to plant them north of the midlands except in those places in the vicinity of the west coast, where the influence of the Gulf Stream is felt. Some grow into large trees whilst others rarely get beyond the bush stage, so it is possible to obtain plants for almost any position. As a rule the best results are obtained in good loamy soil, though one, the Holm Oak, Quercus Ilex, grows remarkably well in poor, sandy or gravelly soil. The specimen shown in the illustration has attained its present dimensions in the poor, hungry soil of Kew. The best species to select are :—

Quercus acuta.—A Japanese bush of sturdy habit, growing 12 to 16 feet high, and as far through, with large, dark green, ovate leaves, which narrow very rapidly near the apex. The larger leaves are upwards of 6 inches long with

HOLM OAK.   IN THE ROYAL GARDENS, KEW

The Evergreen Oaks

stalks 1 inch or more in length. The leaf surface is very glossy.

Q. alnifolia = "Golden Cyprus Oak."—This is an extremely rare species from the mountains of Cyprus. It is of bushy habit and peculiar by reason of its roundish, toothed, Alder-like, leaves, which are of a pretty golden colour on the under side.

Q. Ballota = "Sweet Acorn Oak."—A tall-growing tree from Spain and Portugal. It has dark green, broadly ovate leaves, with sharply-toothed margins. The larger leaves are 2¼ inches long and 1¾ inches wide.

Q. coccifera = "Kermes Oak."—A very slow growing bushy species from the region bordering the Mediterranean. It is of dense shrubby habit, with small, ovate, spiny leaves.

Q. cuspidata.—A Japanese plant with glossy, ovate-acuminate leaves. It rarely gets beyond the dimensions of a spreading bush 10 feet or so high. There is a variety with variegated leaves.

Q. glabra. — This is a handsome Japanese Oak of bush-like habit, with large obovate leaves, dark green and glossy above, and greyish beneath. It forms a large and handsome bush.

Q. Ilex.—For general purposes this is by far the most useful of the group. It is the Holm or Holly Oak of the Mediterranean region, and is met with as a large tree with a clear trunk of 30 feet or more, or again as a tree of medium height

Holly, Yew and Box

with a short thick trunk surmounted by an enormous head of branches. Under either condition it is an imposing tree. The leafage is always dense, consequently it is an ideal plant to use for the purpose of screening or blocking out undesirable objects. The leaves vary very much in size and shape, and even on the same tree leaves may be selected which appear entirely different from each other in almost every particular. Some leaves are conspicuous by reason of their deeply serrated, almost spiny, margins, whilst the margins of others are almost entire. The undersurface of some of the leaves is covered with a silvery pubescence, whilst in the case of others the pubescence is scarcely discernible. Occasionally the foliage is narrow and willow-like, whilst again it may be broadly ovate or almost round. Usually the size may be said to vary from 3 to 4 inches in length and from ¾ to 1 inch in width. The variation in character has been taken advantage of by nurserymen and others, and a number of named varieties are in commerce. Owing to the fact of its being amenable to pruning, the practice has been adopted in some places of keeping it clipped into large, round or pyramidal specimens; when treated in this way, however, the tree loses all its dignity of appearance. In some instances it is used as a hedge plant and as such answers well. Reference has previously been made to its

The Evergreen Oaks

good qualities as a plant for poor, sandy soil, whilst as a seaside tree it is a desirable subject. It has one defect, and that is its dislike to root disturbance. The best plan to adopt is to place the plants in permanent positions when first put out, and use small examples only. The best times to plant are September and May, and the treatment recommended for Hollies may be given. A few of the most distinct varieties are :—Fordii, distinguished by its narrow leaves ; Genabii, remarkable for its bold, handsome foliage; latifolia, with broad, almost round, leaves; and macrophylla, with large and wide leaves.

Q. phillyræoides.—This is a Japanese species of dense, bushy habit, with dark green, oval, serrate leaves on tiny stalks. The larger leaves are 3 inches long and $1\frac{1}{4}$ inches wide. It forms a bush at least 15 feet high about London, but is not of rapid growth. A variety called crispa has been noted. This has curiously crinkled or crisped leaves.

In addition to those already mentioned, the following have evergreen foliage :—Q. agrifolia, a Californian tree ; Q. chrysolepis, the " Maul Oak " from California, a species with a golden under-surface to the leaves ; Q. densiflora, " Tan Bark Oak," California, a large growing tree at home but not of rapid growth at Kew, though it looks like forming a nice tree in time.

Holly, Yew and Box

The Ivies

The Ivies form an important group of evergreen shrubs which thrive almost anywhere and are always presentable. All the known sorts are included under one specific name, though some scientists say that one variety, himalaica, should be given specific rank. The genus to which the Ivies belong is known as Hedera, the species Helix, whilst the natural order is Araliaceæ. The "Common Ivy" together with its numerous varieties is found growing in two totally distinct ways, one, the juvenile stage, as a creeping or climbing plant, and the other, the adult stage, as a stiff, dense bush. The latter stage is usually attained after a plant has reached the top of its support. This variability has been taken advantage of by horticulturists and a distinct set of bushes have been obtained which are distinguished from the climbing varieties by the title of " Bush or Tree Ivies." In form and leaf colouring the Ivy is almost as variable as the Holly, for it differs to a very marked degree. In some instances the leaves are very tiny, being scarcely an inch across, whilst at other times they are 6 inches or more in diameter. The outline also differs to a great extent, for in some cases it is divided to form a number of long narrow segments, whilst again the margins are divided into several large

The Ivies

lobes and sometimes they are almost or quite entire. Colour also shows remarkable variation, numerous shades of green occurring, whilst silver and gold variegation is common.

The leaves of each variety on attaining the adult stage differ in form, and sometimes in colour, from what they were in the juvenile state, and the number of named varieties in commerce is legion. The fruit has also been the means of varietal names being given, for whilst the normal colour is black, varieties are known with yellow and red fruits. The Ivies are suitable for all sorts of work. For covering walls in good positions the choicer varieties are of value ; for rough work, high walls in town or country, the strong growing form known as " Irish Ivy " is invaluable, whilst both this and the type are excellent for clothing ground beneath the shade of trees. Planted against posts, all the climbing sorts form fine pillars of green, silver, or gold, whilst they also look well when covering old tree roots. The " Tree Ivies," on the other hand, are excellent for forming groups or beds, whilst they are also of service for decorative work when grown in pots. Ivies thrive in almost any kind of soil, light loam suiting them perhaps best. When grown against walls it is advisable to go over them in April each year and clip them well back, otherwise they grow out from the wall and become unsafe. When grown for picturesque-

Holly, Yew and Box

ness on ruins, etc., this cutting back should be dispensed with. Varieties that show a disposition to revert to the type should be gone over once or twice a year and have all pieces removed that are going astray.

Select list of climbing varieties.

Large-leaved green.—algeriensis, amurensis, azorica, canariensis (Irish Ivy), colchica, dentata, gigantea.

Other green-leaved varieties. — angularis, Cænwoodiana, crenata, deltoidea, digitata, donerailensis, Emerald Green, lucida, minima, minor, nigra, ovata, sagittæfolia, triloba, venosa.

Silver-leaved varieties.—algeriensis variegata, Crippsii, maculata, maderensis variegata, marginata major, marginata media, marmorata elegans, minor variegata.

Gold-leaved varieties.—angularis foliis aureis, canariensis aureo-maculata, Cavendishi, chrysomela, chrysophylla, farleyensis, flavescens, palmata aurea.

Bush or Tree varieties.

Green-leaved. — aborescens, arborescens heidelbergensis and a. Rægneriana.

Silver-leaved. — arborescens foliis argenteis marginatis, Silver Queen, algeriensis variegata (tree form).

Gold-leaved. — arborescens foliis aureis, and tree forms of other gold-leaved sorts.

XXVIII

THE LAURELS

THE name of Laurel with one or another prefix is applied to several very different shrubs, all of which are evergreen and occupy an important position in gardens. The principal ones are the " Common or Cherry Laurel," Prunus Laurocerasus ; the " Portugal Laurel," Prunus lusitanica ; the " Bay Laurel," Laurus nobilis ; the " Sheep Laurel," Kalmia angustifolia ; the " Alexandrian Laurel," Danæa Laurus ; the " Spurge Laurel," Daphne Laureola ; the " Great Laurel," Rhododendron maximum. Of this number the three first mentioned are of the greatest service

The Common Laurel = " Prunus Laurocerasus." —Although of late years it has become the custom to heap abuse on the "Common Laurel," and generally decry its culture, this has been carried too far, and if people would only apply their abuse to the absurd way in which the plant is too often treated and recommend more rational methods of culture it would be far more to the point. The fact of its being of a peculiarly accommodating nature, lending itself readily to all kinds of work, coupled with the fact that it

Holly, Yew and Box

can be propagated easily and procured cheaply,
caused people to use it at every turn whether in
or out of keeping with the surroundings and
without thought as to its ultimate suitability for
those positions.   Thus whole shrubberies were
planted with the one thing, and as the plants grew
out of bounds they were regularly clipped back,
thus destroying the natural outline of the shrub.
Such effects were certainly deplorable, but the
same shrub grown in a natural way is a very
different object.   When placed singly with plenty
of room for development the " Common Laurel "
forms a bush 16 or 18 feet high, and more across,
with large, leathery, deep green leaves and
axillary inflorescences 4 or 5 inches long of white
flowers, which are succeeded by deep purple or
black fruits.   The accompanying illustration is of
such a plant, but unfortunately the photograph
could not be taken when the plant was in flower.
P. Laurocerasus is a native of Eastern Europe
and the Orient, and in addition to the type a
number of varieties are known which differ in
size of foliage and stature.   The best of these
are :—caucasica, colchica, compacta, latifolia,
magnoliæfolia, Otinii, rotundifolia, schipkaensis,
versaillensis.

The variety magnoliæfolia is a very vigorous
grower with large leaves ; it can, with a little
training be induced to assume a tree-like habit
with a fair-sized trunk.   Otinii is remarkable for

The Laurels

its large, oval, dark green leaves, and schipkænsis
for its narrow foliage. Varieties are known with
variegated and malformed leaves, but they are of
no decorative value. The leaves of the " Common
Laurel " have sometimes been used for flavouring
purposes in mistake for those of the " Bay Laurel "
with disastrous results for they contain prussic
acid.

The Portugal Laurel.—This, Prunus lusitanica,
like the foregoing plant is included in the
Laurocerasus group of the genus Prunus. It is
found in Spain and Portugal, and grows into a
large bush, sometimes 20 feet high and as much
across, with a trunk a foot or so in diameter. It
is really less striking than the " Common Laurel,"
but is well worth growing, its oblong leaves being
very dark in colour, against which the racemes
of white flowers during early summer contrast
admirably. There are varieties known under the
names of azorica, coriacea, myrtifolia, ormstoniensis and variegata. Of these myrtifolia, with
small leaves and compact habit, and ormstoniensis
with larger leaves than the type, are the most
distinct. The " Portugal Laurels " are bad
subjects to transplant; the best time to perform
the work is May or September, and intending
planters should be contented by procuring small,
young specimens not more than 2 or 2½ feet high,
for if cajoled into purchasing large, old plants
they will probably lose five out of six.

Holly, Yew and Box

The Bay Laurel.—In addition to this name Laurus nobilis is known under several others, such as, "Sweet Bay," "Poet's Laurel," and "Roman Laurel." It is really the true Laurel, and the plant used so extensively by the Greeks and Romans in classical times, for twining into wreaths wherewith to crown their heroes, probably through this reason the names of Poet's and Roman Laurel were given. It belongs to the order Lauraceæ, a family peculiar for the number of more or less fragrant leaved plants it contains. In the colder counties it is not very hardy, but fine examples are met with from the midlands southwards. At Margam Park, Port Talbot, it assumes very large proportions, many trees being upward of 40 feet high and as far across. The leaves are more or less oval but acuminate at both ends, bright green, 3 to 5 inches long and 1 to 1½ inches wide. They contain an aromatic essence, which is made use of by cooks for flavouring purposes. A small leaved variety is known under the name of angustifolia; it is of neat address. At Osborne, I.W., several specimens of a small foliaged variety may be seen which have curiously wrinkled margins to the leaves. Laurus nobilis is a native of the Mediterranean region.

The Sheep Laurel.—This is a North American shrub belonging to Ericaceæ. Its correct name is Kalmia angustifolia, and it forms

COMMON LAUREL, PRUNUS LAUROCERASUS

The Laurels

a many branched shrub 18 inches or so high, spreading rapidly under favourable conditions by means of underground stems. The leaves are small and it cannot be called a really useful evergreen; it is, however, worth growing in any garden where peat-loving plants thrive on account of its pretty, rose-coloured flowers, which appear in May and June. There are several varieties which differ chiefly in stature.

The Alexandrian Laurel.—Danæa Laurus is a near relative of the "Butcher's Broom," Ruscus aculeatus, in fact it has been known as Ruscus racemosus. It grows to a height of 2 feet or so and is of a pleasing shade of green. The flowers are inconspicuous, but it bears ornamental red fruits. For shady places it is an excellent plant.

The Spurge Laurel. — This plant, Daphne Laureola, forms a spreading bush 3 feet high with evergreen leaves and fragrant, greenish yellow flowers, which appear in spring. It is a native of Europe, N. Africa, and W. Asia, and thrives in loamy soil in which lime is found.

The Great Laurel.—A large growing Rhododendron from N. America, which is also known as the "American Rose Bay." The correct name is R. maximum. It forms a large bush up to 15 feet or so in height, with handsome oblong leaves and large heads of reddish flowers. Cultivation is similar to that of other Rhododendrons.

XXIX

OTHER EVERGREENS

ARCTOSTAPHYLOS. — The best known species is Uva - ursi, a prostrate-habited, pink-flowered shrub, suitable for planting to hang over rockwork or for covering banks. A. Manzanita is a Californian shrub with rounded Eucalyptus-like leaves. The flowers are pink and borne in terminal corymbs in spring. It ought not to be planted in exposed places.

Aucuba japonica is a well-known shrub which attains a height of 6 or 8 feet. The leaves are glossy and Laurel-like, those of the type being green, and those of various varieties golden variegated. Male and female flowers are. borne on separate plants, and by planting both sexes together very ornamental fruiting plants are obtained, the fruits being red and retained throughout winter. It is the most useful of all shrubs for planting in dense, shady places, as it thrives in places where most other things fail. It also grows well in full sun.

Azara microphylla is an elegant, Chilian shrub, which grows at least 20 feet high, bearing small, deep green leaves and white flowers.

Other Evergreens

Berberis.—Several species and varieties are excellent evergreens whilst some are first rate flowering shrubs. B. stenophylla is possibly the most useful shrub we possess for all round purposes, whilst B. Darwinii and B. Wallichiana are also first rate evergreen and flowering plants. The Mahonia section is also of great value, the chief species being B. Aquifolium, japonica, nepalensis, and repens.

Buxus, see Box.

Calluna, see Heaths, etc.

Camellia japonica. — This shrub is hardier than many people give it credit for, and when well grown it is an extremely ornamental evergreen which has the advantage of being a good flowerer. Most of the varieties usually grown indoors may be planted out of doors in the warmer parts of the midlands.

Cassinia. — Small leaved shrubs of rather straggling growth if not kept well knifed in whilst young. C. fulvida, with golden variegated leaves, and C. leptophylla, with silvery leaves, are the most useful.

Castanopsis chrysophylla = the "Golden-leaved Chestnut." — This is a close relative of the Sweet Chestnut, having similar shaped but much smaller fruits. It forms a small tree with leaves very like those of the Holm Oak in shape, but the reverse side is of a pretty golden colour.

Cotoneaster. — The principal evergreen

species are angustifolia, buxifolia, microphylla and thymifolia. The first-mentioned plant requires wall culture in most places.

Cratægus Pyracantha.—This is well known as the orange-scarlet fruited Pyracantha so often grown against walls. It is, however, quite hardy and thrives as a bush in the open. Several varieties are known, including one with white fruits, and another with larger fruits than the type called Lalandi. A companion species is C. crenulata.

Cistus. — The various Cistuses are capital plants for clothing dry sunny banks, and they thrive in poor soil. Most of the species are rather tender, but several withstand ordinary winters about London. All are very floriferous and blossom during May and June. Good ones are corbariensis, crispus, ladaniferus, laurifolius, purpureus, and villosus.

Daphne. — The " Spurge Laurel," Daphne Laureola, has already been mentioned. In addition we have D. pontica, a rather large-leaved shrub growing 4 feet or so high ; D. Laureola Philippi, dwarfer and bearing smaller leaves than the type ; D. L. purpurea, with purplish leaves ; D. oleoides, a small leaved purple flowered plant ; D. Cneorum, the "Garland Flower," a dwarf plant with tiny leaves and pretty, fragrant light red flowers ; and others.

Daphniphyllum macropodum. — A large growing shrub from China and Japan, with fine

Other Evergreens

Laurel-like foliage. It attains a height of 8 feet with a similar diameter. The variety jezœnsis is of dwarf, compact habit.

Elæagnus.—Several species grow into ornamental bushes of great size. E. glabra forms a large bush quite 10 feet high and as far through with glossy green leaves. E. pungens is a similar looking shrub. Of this there are numerous varieties with golden variegated leaves; the best one is called Simonii. Another good evergreen species is macrophylla; this has broad silvery leaves which are very effective.

Empetrum nigrum is the "Crowberry" of the north temperate and arctic zones. It is a neat growing evergreen, forming a dense carpet a few inches high.

Escallonia.—Several species are suitable for the Southern counties, or for walls further north. E. macrantha, with red flowers, is the most useful species to use as an evergreen.

Eucryphia pinnatifolia. — This is one of the choicest of all shrubs, its large Camellia-like white flowers being the chief attraction. In some places it proves evergreen and in others semi-deciduous.

Euonymus. — The various golden and silver variegated forms of E. japonicus and E. radicans, together with the type of each, are useful evergreens. E. radicans thrives well beneath trees.

Gaultheria procumbens is a low growing shrub

suitable for carpeting beds. G. Shallon grows to a height of 6 or 8 feet, sometimes more, and forms a large mass. It is a good subject for undergrowth.

Helianthemum.—The various Helianthemums or Rock Roses are suitable for sunny banks; they thrive in almost any kind of soil. Of H. vulgare there are very many varieties.

Kalmia latifolia.—A handsome, Rhododendron-like shrub with large, dark green leaves, and heads of white, pink tinged flowers. Cultivation similar to Rhododendron.

Ledum latifolium and palustre are a couple of dense growing peat-loving shrubs, which have rather small leaves and white flowers.

Ligustrum. — This genus is represented in gardens by the numerous Privets; good evergreen species are japonicum, lucidum, ovalifolium and its golden form, and strongylophyllum.

Magnolia grandiflora is well known by reason of its immense, handsome, leathery leaves, and large white, fragrant flowers. About London and further south it thrives as a bush in the open, further north it should be planted against a wall.

Osmanthus Aquifolium is a very distinct, Holly-like, evergreen, of dense habit, suitable for forming beds in prominent positions. There are numerous varieties, of which ilicifolius, ilicifolius purpureus, and ilicifolius variegatus are the most useful.

Other Evergreens

Pernettya mucronata forms a dense growing shrub 2 to 3 feet high, with tiny leaves and white flowers, followed by ornamental fruits which ripen in autumn. The fruits are red, purple, pink or white in colour.

Phillyræa.—A useful genus of evergreen shrubs allied to the Privets. Several sorts grow into very large and ornamental bushes. The best are P. angustifolia and variety rosmarinifolia, P. decora, P. latifolia, and P. media.

Pieris. — A genus allied to the Heaths and kindred plants, all of which require the same conditions. Three useful species are grown, floribunda, japonica, and formosa. The latter is tender and is unsuitable for any but the milder counties.

Rhamnus Alaternus grows into a large bush, but is not of special interest. The variety angustifolia has small leaves and is of rather dwarf habit. A form of this with silver variegated leaves is a distinct and pretty shrub.

Rosmarinus officinalis.—This is well known as the " Rosemary." It is usually grown on account of its fragrance.

Ruscus.—The various members of this family are useful shade plants. All are comparatively dwarf growers. The best are R. aculeatus, the " Butcher's Broom," and R. Hypoglossum.

Veronica. — The numerous species of New Zealand, shrubby Veronicas are suitable for the warmer counties. V. Traversii is the hardiest of all and thrives well north of London.

Viburnum.—The best known evergreen species of this genus is V. Tinus the Laurustinus. It is a valuable winter flowering plant which thrives in all except the very coldest parts of the country. A new evergreen species is V. rhytido-phyllum from China.

Yucca. — The various hardy Yuccas are all valuable evergreens as they strike a distinct note of change from everything else in the garden. The most useful are Y. angustifolia, of dwarf habit, with small, narrow leaves ; Y. gloriosa, of larger growth with stiff upright leaves ; and Y. recurvifolia with semi-pendant foliage.

Through lack of space I have been unable to refer to all the hardy evergreens, and have not been able to do more than briefly refer to others. This was unavoidable as the work was intended to deal directly with the Holly, Yew, and Box only, the other notes being appended to direct attention to the many serviceable evergreens, suitable for gardens in any but the very coldest parts of the country.

INDEX

INDEX

PART I.—THE HOLLY

277

Holly, Yew and Box

278

Index

Index

PART II.—THE YEW

Holly, Yew and Box

PART III.—THE BOX

Index

PART IV.—OTHER EVERGREENS

Holly, Yew and Box